INNER PRACTICES

FOR THE

TWELVE

NIGHTS

OF

YULETIDE

Anne Stallkamp

Werner Hartung

EARTHDANCER

AN INNER TRADITIONS IMPRINT

First edition 2021, reprinted 2021
Inner Practices for the Twelve Nights of Yuletide
Anne Stallkamp, Werner Hartung

This English edition © 2021 Earthdancer GmbH
English translation © 2021 JMS books LLP
Editing by JMS books LLP (www.jmseditorial.com)

Originally published in German as: *Rauhnaechte, Zeit für mich*
World © 2014, Neue Erde GmbH, Saarbruecken, Germany

Cover design: DesignIsIdentity.com
Cover images: full moon: Claudio Divizia; ornaments and background: rvika;
snowflakes: ch123; all shutterstock.
Typesetting and layout: Chris Bell
Typeset in ITC Novarese
Printed and bound in the United States by Integrated Books International

ISBN 978-1-64411-324-0 (print)
ISBN 978-1-64411-325-7 (ebook)

Published by Earthdancer, an imprint of Inner Traditions
www.earthdancerbooks.com, www.innertraditions.com

Winter Harvest

The oilseed rape boldly braves
The winter storms and sleet
That seek to mow it down,
Level with the ground.

Four crop rotations
In a year, this time around.
Mild weather rules December
Before the harvest of the Nights of Yuletide.

Spring was too cold,
Summer and fall too dry.
No rain set in to soak
All that cried out for ripening.

Reach for fruition now,
As light returns.
This year has caused you
Hunger and thirst.

The full moon brings
Cold and clarity;
Turn your life to follow
The path of the sun.

Werner Hartung

Contents

PART ONE
Understanding the Nights of Yuletide

1. Time: The Rhythm of Existence   9

2. Significance of the Twelve Nights of Yuletide   13
   Twelve magical nights: The year's great pause   13
   Channeling Minerva: The Nights of Yuletide   14
   Counting the days: Endings and beginnings   16
   Topics and themes to consider: Looking back, looking
   ahead, and being receptive to the qualities of time as
   a way to self-assurance   16

3. Looking Back   19
   The past and letting go   19
   Personal retrospection during the Twelve Nights of Yuletide   19

4. Looking Ahead   21
   The New Year and experiencing the new   21
   Personal reflection on the future during the Twelve Nights
   of Yuletide   22

5. Resolution Ritual for the Yuletide Season   25

6. The Twelve Nights of Yuletide   27
   Perceiving the quality of time   27
   Introduction to the practical exercises   28
   Meditations   29

PART TWO
Themes and Time Qualities of the Twelve Nights of Yuletide

First Night of Yuletide (December 21/22)
Sense the quality of time   33

Second Night of Yuletide (December 22/23)
Find humility and devotion   45

Third Night of Yuletide (December 23/24)
Discover the power of your heart   53

Fourth Night of Yuletide (December 24/25)
Find peace   61

Fifth Night of Yuletide (December 25/26)
Embrace trust   73

Sixth Night of Yuletide (December 26/27)
Discover tranquility   81

Seventh Night of Yuletide (December 27/28)
Self-care   89

Eighth Night of Yuletide (December 28/29)
Truth and clarity   97

Ninth Night of Yuletide (December 29/30)
Serenity   105

Tenth Night of Yuletide (December 30/31)
Journey into a new life   115

Eleventh Night of Yuletide (December 31/January 1)
Explore your feelings anew   123

Twelfth Night of Yuletide (January 1/2)
Be creative in shaping and achieving the life you want   131

Returning to Your Daily Routine (January 2/3)
Embracing and enjoying life   139

About the authors   143

PART ONE

———⟨◆⟩———

Understanding the Nights of Yuletide

ONE

Time: The Rhythm of Existence

Let's start with the key question: What is time?

Time is imperceptible without rhythm.

When we talk about "rhythm" in everyday speech, it refers to the alternation between tension and release: cardiac rhythm, the rhythm of the tides, our daily rhythm, our work rhythm, even the rhythm of a painting.

Rhythm is music's pattern of sound, silence, and emphasis in time, from nuances in volume, note duration, and tempo. Rhythm occurs in nature and the arts (poetry, painting, architecture, sculpture). In linguistics, it is the phrasing of language through the interchange of syllables—long and short, accented and unaccented—and of pauses and cadence. Rhythm can also mean symmetry, equally arranged movement, periodic change, and regular recurrence.

What are our temporal rhythms? What structures and provides a pattern for our time, making our temporal rhythms tangible?

An average inhalation lasts for three seconds. Each breath provides rhythm; there is a small pause between inhaling and exhaling. We cannot take a breath in advance or catch up on a missed breath. Each breath occurs in the present. Our breath is now.

We blink every six seconds. The action of blinking adds rhythm to our sight; it is the breath of the soul.

An hour is sufficient time for a deep and meaningful encounter with another person.

There are 2 x 12 hours in a day, comprising day and night: 3 (the number of Heaven) x 4 (the number of the Earth) = 12 (the number of the divine rays of light). Dusk and dawn are the day's times of transition, its thresholds. They amplify our spiritual and mental powers and boost our intuition (the so-called "blue hour"). The doors to other worlds are thrown open.

This echoes many spiritual traditions in which evening and dusk are seen as times when people can open themselves up to their emotions and moods (and to the powers that act upon them) more effectively than during the bustle of the day. Falling asleep and waking up are also threshold stages, times of transition in which psychological and spiritual questions and answers are close at hand.

Comprising 7 days (3 + 4), a week corresponds to one quarter of a moon phase; all humanity lives according to this rhythm of 7. Each week repeats the basic energy qualities of the divine rays of light. The number 6 or the six-pointed star correspond to the perfected human being, the highest state that human beings can achieve (2 x 3 = 6 days + 1 day of rest after the Creation = 7 days of the week). Each successive day begins on the evening of the preceding day.

Saturday is the eve of Sunday. The week shapes the rhythm of the soul.

A month of 4 x 7 = 28 days corresponds to the phases of the moon, a cycle of waxing and waning.

A year has 4 seasons, each one of which has 3 months: 4 x 3 = 12 months, divided by the solstices as holy days, thresholds, and periods of transition:

March 21   Spring equinox (Ostara/Alban Eiler, Christian Easter)

June 21   Summer solstice, longest day of the year, Midsummer (Litha/Alban Hefyn, Christian Feast of St John on June 24)

September 21   Autumnal equinox (Mabon/Alban Elved, Harvest Festival, Christian Michaelmas on September 29)

December 21   Winter solstice, longest night of the year (Yule/Alban Arthan, Christian Christmas Eve on December 24)

As we can see, the Christian festivals are offset from the actual dates of the holy days by three or more days; this is because they are solar festivals, determined by the course of the sun.

The Celtic lunar festivals are correspondingly diagonally offset from these throughout the year:

February 1 – 2	(Celtic Imbolc, Christian Candlemas on February 2)
April 30 – May 1	(Celtic Beltane, Walpurgis Night, on May 1)
July 31 – August 1	(Celtic Lughnasadh, Lammas, on August 1)
October 31 – November 1	(Celtic Samhain, Christian All Saints' Day/ All Hallows' on November 1/2)

The twelve magical nights of the Yuletide season equate to the time difference between the solar and lunar years, the interval "between the years." This is the great pause in the rhythm of the year. A single great festival, a threshold, a time of transition, a moment in which to stop and take stock (in centuries past everything came to a halt during this period) and yet simultaneously a time for looking ahead to the coming year.

Since the invention of artificial light in 1880 (just over 140 years ago), we are no longer bound by the rhythms of day and night, sun and moon. During this time, we have, in particular, strayed from the rhythms of the sun and moon with their equinoxes and solstices that occur through the year.

In addition, in the Western world, we now have access to everything 24/7. We no longer have to hope for a good harvest that will see us through the winter, so our opportunity—indeed our responsibility— to turn our attention to the spiritual world is greater than ever. The question we face today is whether our spiritual light (our spiritual "harvest") will also see us through several or even just one dark time. We need to cast our minds back to the powers of Creation, not just in the place in which we find ourselves but in space and time, and their zenith.

My Breath

In my deepest dreams
The Earth weeps
Blood
Stars laugh
In my eyes

If people come to me
With multicolored questions,
I answer:
Go ask Socrates
The past
Has created me
I have
Inherited the future

My breath means
Now

Rose Ausländer

TWO

Significance of the Twelve Nights of Yuletide

Twelve magical nights: The year's great pause

The nights between the winter solstice (December 21) and January 3 (sometimes January 6) are known in various traditions as the Nights of Yuletide (also as Twelvetide in the English-speaking world, or Raunacht (night of yule) in Germany, jul in Sweden, Denmark, and Norway, and jól in Iceland). Customs and mythology ascribe particular significance to this period when time "stands still," while the literature assigns wildly differing times to the actual beginning and end of this period. There are also many different interpretations of the period's origins, nature, customs, and rituals, but we do not intend to detain ourselves further with its traditions here.

In December 2010, we were lucky enough to receive through Minerva and Werner a channeled message recalling the original intentions and the "correct" timeframe (*see overleaf*).

Channeling Minerva: The Nights of Yuletide

I am Minerva. I was worshiped in Rome as the goddess of practical and artisanal knowledge, but I am no goddess, nor ever was one. There is only One God! I am one of the Elohim* and I help Jophiel with the great task of imparting the knowledge and wisdom of the universe to you in practical ways that are relevant to your lives.

We Elohim restrict ourselves to the knowledge that originates on this Earth as, like you, we serve Gaia. We also serve you as the race that protects her. How nice it would be if you could, in the near future, find time to discover more about us, receive our message, and ask us questions, which we will gladly answer.

Werner, how wonderful it is to answer your question about what really lies behind the so-called Nights of Yuletide. You are quite right in feeling that, here too, matters are more straightforward than your mythologies, customs, and religions might make out. And the literature about them also complicates things far too much.

You like to call this period the "fifth season" or, if you jokingly include Carnival, the sixth. The "time between the years" is indeed a fifth season, an energetic buffer zone, as far as its time quality is concerned, that is unlike any other transition or turning point. Archangel Uriel, whose duties include managing the qualities of time, has given you an opportunity in this period to train your perceptive abilities and to learn how to sense the messages offered by this window in time.

In your calendar, this period commences during the night of December 21/22 and concludes with the night of January 2/3, irrespective of other influences that tradition tells you might be involved and which you should disregard.

---

* The Elohim are energetic beings, intelligences with higher powers who guide us humans as the guardian race of the planet Gaia. This happens on an individual basis according to the "area of interest" each represents, and in each case they are associated with the spheres of activity of the twelve Archangels. They amplify and transform their energies through their "interdimensional" position between Heaven and Earth; this explains the immense power that many people feel when they come into contact with them (and which can lead people to conclude that the Elohim are "higher" than the Archangels). The Elohim are also guardians of certain parts of the Earth's natural world and of the elements. Through the concept of science, Minerva is associated with the Archangel Jophiel (wisdom, enlightenment).

However, what is relevant is understanding that these twelve days will act like a movie trailer for the qualities of the twelve months to come. In this way we can picture our lives in advance before events actually occur, as if they were taking place in a film, which can help with making decisions. Some people are aware that by carefully observing the weather during the Nights of Yuletide (a term that should also include all dark days in general!), they can draw certain conclusions about what the weather will be like during the coming year. And how right they are.

However, this is by no means everything. If you pause to examine your feelings and open yourself up during this period, you will have access to the most important insights about the twelve months to come and can prepare yourself mentally for the themes to be considered, the qualities of time, and the challenges.

Begin each day (remember to start the evening before) by asking yourself what you have yet to work through or what you have yet to forgive yourself or others for. Replay the lessons and experiences of the year that has just passed in your mind, like life flashing before your eyes. Each year represents a new beginning, a new quality, a new opportunity for growth. Will you make the most of this? Have you, indeed, even really been aware of it? When else can you take a break to think and reflect if not during these mysterious nights in which the transition from darkness to light is gradually completed. Just as each night is a time of rest before greeting the new day, you can use the "long night" of these twelve days to prepare for a whole year.

Take a deep breath and reenergize. Spend the daylight hours on long walks and the long hours of darkness in meditation and sleep. Bring some order to your thoughts and feelings, make plans, both alone and with others, but also be merry and celebrate.

None of these days will be as any other, and nor should they be. Explore them with your feelings and emotions, and you will discover how to receive and interpret their revelations. We will be happy to help you: we Elohim, the natural spirits, and the whole spiritual world. Take the time to look and reenergize before greeting the New Year with confidence and a heart full of hope

Greetings from us, the Elohim
A message from Minerva

Counting the days: Endings and beginnings

As described earlier, each successive day begins on the evening of the preceding day. As Minerva points out, the Nights of Yuletide begin at dusk with the first night, December 21, ushering in the darkness of the longest night of the year, which is succeeded by the second night, as evening falls on December 22.

To be absolutely precise, the duration of the Yuletide season is in fact thirteen days. The twelve Yuletide nights and the energy qualities and themes associated with them end with the Twelfth Night of Yuletide, January 2, which itself begins on the evening of January 1.

The Thirteenth night, January 2/3, represents the threshold of our return from "stopped" time to playing an active and creative role in shaping life, although time continues to "stand still" on this day, too.

Thirteen is the number of God (Three in One and One in Three) and his Creation in the trinity of thought, word, and deed. The meditation on this night thus serves as a final affirmation of self before returning to our daily lives.

Given the busy time in the lead up to the Christmas holidays, the beginning of this period might not appear to be the most convenient moment in which to take some time out to explore our feelings (and this might also be the reason why many people see December 24 as the start of the Yuletide celebrations), but in fact it is particularly suitable. Ultimately, each person can approach it as they see fit. We can only pass on the recommendations of the spiritual world as we have received and experienced them for ourselves.

Topics and themes to consider: Looking back, looking ahead, and being receptive to the qualities of time as a way to self-assurance

There are three essential areas on which we can focus during this period. The Twelve Nights of Yuletide provide an opportunity for us to look back and close the book on the past. We can also look ahead to the topics, themes and events for the year to come, even including the weather, as each Yuletide night is associated with a different month of the coming year. What is less well known is that the twelve nights/days each have their own quality of time, when we are particularly sensitive to a specific topic or theme; when we reflect upon this theme during this period, we gain a better spiritual understanding of it. It can serve as a kind of "training program" for our self-assurance.

Below is a summary of the Twelve Nights of Yuletide as they relate to the themes for self-reflection and contemplation, the months of the year, and the transition periods for looking forward and backward.

Night of Yuletide	Theme	Date	Festival/ Threshold
1 December 21/22	Time quality	January 1	
2 December 22/23	Humility, devotion	February 1	Imbolc
3 December 23/24	The power of the heart	March 21	Spring equinox
4 December 24/25	Peace	April 30	Beltane
5 December 25/26	Trust	May 1	
6 December 26/27	Tranquility	June 21	Summer solstice
7 December 27/28	Taking care of yourself	July 31	Lughnasadh
8 December 28/29	Truth/clarity	August 1	
9 December 29/30	Serenity	September 21	Autumn equinox
10 December 30/31	New life	October 31	Samhain
11 December 31/ January 1	Exploring your feelings	November 1	
12 January 1/2	Inventive creativity	December 21	Winter solstice

THREE

Looking Back

The past and letting go

As the old year finishes and we look back, we are aware of something coming to an end, while the new year signals the start of something that is to be welcomed with joy. It is not a question of condemning the past year or seeing it through rose-colored glasses, or indeed of becoming emotional about things that have happened. The key is to recognize and seize this opportunity, revisiting every wrong decision and resolving situations that have gone awry. By looking back, we can also make use of the healing energy or *reiki* that we send out to past events to transform them for the present. In this way, we can resolve old patterns of behavior, free ourselves from any issues in which we have become embroiled, and create space for new things, for what we desire, and for healing.

Personal retrospection during the Twelve Nights of Yuletide

How should you look back over the year?

One option is to conduct a personal review of the old year, month by month, based on the Nights of Yuletide.

You will have special memories of celebrations such as birthdays, but you might also remember other events, mundane or more significant, that were less pleasant.

You might also incorporate the questions and rituals for the theme of the day into your review, asking yourself how you dealt with that day's theme over the course of the past year and thinking about what you did well and not so well. You will find that Part Two features some helpful questions in this respect.

Round off each session of reflection on the year gone by with a short prayer in which you first forgive yourself and then others, before giving thanks for all the support you have received and the good things you have experienced.

FOUR

Looking Ahead

The New Year and experiencing the new

Human beings have always been inquisitive; despite our very best intentions to be satisfied with being present in the moment, what we really want to know (in as much detail as possible!) is what awaits us around the corner. Take the weather. There are few predictions as well refined as weather forecasts and yet look how often the weather surprises us. This teaches us that although it is indeed possible to predict trends and perhaps even some certainties, such as the arrival of a hurricane, even a hurricane can change course at the last minute, wreaking havoc in a different area from the one predicted, or sparing another originally thought to have been in its path.

Similarly, not everything is predestined in people's lives, despite a life plan that was set before birth. This includes the lessons required by karma and those we impose upon ourselves, as well as our encounters with certain people, which do not occur by chance.

God is omnipotent and yet He compels us to follow our life plan as little as He compels a storm to follow a particular path; the energy of our souls is a part of divine energy, released for a certain time by the Creator as part of Creation in miniature, as we devise and live out our small realities within the greater work of the cosmos.

Our right to existence is based on creating and acting on the promptings of the love in our hearts, but this includes the freedom to deviate from a plan when we feel things differently and even the freedom to leave the path of love.

Predictions and prophecies have only limited value if they are solicited or are provided on condition that they will be completely accurate.

In the worst cases, we then merely establish a pseudo-certainty from third parties, which, with our scant or total lack of self-confidence, we view as infallible. This entails considerable risk, including the danger of misconceptions and misinterpretations concerning astrology and clairvoyance and the opportunities presented by channeling.

We mention this in advance to ensure that you view your contemplation of the year ahead in the correct light and that it makes sense. Things you "see" in dreams or in a waking state may come to pass, but equally they may not; they are showing you topics or themes and events for which the time is becoming right or "ripe," as far as anyone can anticipate. The date estimated for a person's life-changing event may well alter and some events may not occur at all or will take place in a different way; the intentions and behavior of the people involved are often too difficult to predict with any certainty.

Personal reflection on the future during the Twelve Nights of Yuletide

One way of having some perspective on the coming year is by thinking about what we wish and hope for, writing it down, and daydreaming about it or visualizing it taking place.

What should you do with the insights and feelings you have during the Yuletide nights? You could write down your ideas or ambitions for the future in a special journal. Or you could depict them in a painting or make them into a collage that you keep in your journal.

Try to make a note of any daydreams relating to the future as soon as you have had them. Then wait a little, to give yourself some distance from them, before adding a note of your thoughts and feelings about these daydreams, along with any insights and desires concerning how you are going to deal with the time quality (theme) of that particular day. Prepare your own affirmations to work with in the months to come.

Remember also that the veil to the other world has been lifted and the doors are open. In other words, we have easier access to our unconscious desires and our life plan and can more easily make contact with the beings who wish us well and accompany us on our path: natural beings, spirit guides, ancestors, and power animals.

If we are equally receptive to our nighttime dreams and our feelings and impressions (such as prompted by what and who we encounter walking in the countryside or during meditation), we may be given hints that will guide us one way or another).

Write down your dreams in as much detail as you can remember, including the accompanying feelings and emotions and the associations and thoughts that gave rise to them. Note what you encounter: people and situations, what you see on walks in the countryside (plants and animals, for example), what you see during meditations. You might like to take photos or make a note of them in a drawing or sketch.

Develop an interest in "interpreting" your dreams. Take a quiet moment to do so soon after your dream, but give yourself time to evaluate and interpret what you have seen for the future and discuss it quietly with people you trust. However, remember that it is important not to allow your dream to create any anxiety or fear.

FIVE

Resolution Ritual for the Yuletide Season

What should you do if something goes wrong during the Nights of Yuletide? Perhaps tempers are raised or an action is perceived as harmful. In such eventualities during this special period, do not waste time in trying to resolve restrictive energies, otherwise they will exert an influence on the coming year and the month represented by the relevant Yule night.

The resolution ritual should ideally be conducted by the two individuals involved. Sit down opposite each other or side by side. Place your right hand on the heart chakra of the other person and ask them to do the same to you. Now, take turns to say:

I ask you to forgive me for (briefly describe the reason or occasion).

I forgive myself and I release both you and me from everything that restricts us in this matter.

May all that constrained us be resolved, in the light of the One God, and may that which was divided be united again; so be it.

I thank you for reconciling with me and may you be surrounded by love. Blessings be upon you.

If the other person is not present, spread out your hands and direct your energy to them as you address them with the words above.

SIX

The Twelve Nights of Yuletide

Perceiving the quality of time

While this book was being written, I (Werner) very consciously immersed myself in the energy of the Yuletide nights. The special time qualities of each day were explained to me through the spiritual world, but only after I had sensed them myself, using my own daily themes for meditation. Since then, being sensitive to these qualities has proved their usefulness time and again during our many years of practical work and with many people, often setting in motion processes of profound importance.

Together, the twelve nights and days, each with its own very special theme (one for each night and successive day), form a "program" for self-discovery and self-assurance that you can follow each year, an annual aid for reflection during this period of transition and transformation, which we present in detail here.

Our guide features a description of each theme and time quality for each of the twelve magical nights, along with exercises, meditations, and key questions intended to help you to be open and receptive to the task at hand. It ends with a guide to how to return to your normal everyday life during the thirteenth night. We have suggested some questions, exercises, and meditations for each Yuletide night. Make a conscious decision to select only those elements that really speak to you. There is no need to work through every stage methodically.

Introduction to the practical exercises

As already mentioned, you might like to make a personal journal to accompany your exercises during the nights of the Yuletide season. It can contain all your notes, sketches, and photos and can then be referred to during the year to come.

If possible, time the writing of your entries to begin as dusk falls. Perform a ritual or small celebration, light a candle and make yourself comfortable. Create a pleasant atmosphere and burn some incense with flowers, herbs, and resins. Begin each evening by reading the chapter on the time qualities of the Yuletide night about to commence. You might like to start with a brief review of the day, in which case open your journal and jot down the key events. Establish whether any patterns can be detected behind any less pleasant occurrences and what those patterns might be; make a note of them and write an affirmation about them. Compose a closing prayer: to whom or what are you offering forgiveness or thanks? It could be for particular encounters with individuals or helpful and pleasant events and situations that have arisen. You could paste a relevant photo in your journal or record something with a sketch.

Now devote your attention entirely to the present and the particular theme of the day, considering it carefully and reflecting on how you feel about it.

To prepare for each Yuletide night, we recommend that you use the *Sensing the quality of time* exercise in the First Night of Yuletide section (see page 37). Choose a question, affirmation, or exercise from Part Two (the practical section) and take it with you into the night, into your dreams. When you wake up, meditate upon it and examine how you feel about it; make it part of your life and your experience in the coming day. Keep a note of your choice and record the insights and experiences it brings.

Be alert to the way you feel and attentive to your dreams and daydreams. Record what you have seen or wished for in your dreams in note or image form in your journal. Make a note of the things and people you encounter.

Picture in your mind what you are hoping for in the corresponding month of the year to come. Visualize whatever you are hoping for in the entire year to come in relation to the theme of that particular day, bearing in mind that you are looking at the meaning of the time quality, not just for the corresponding month but for the coming year as a whole. Record what you have visualized in note form and/or as images. Prepare affirmations that you can work with over the next few months.

These notes and records should prove invaluable in the year to come. When difficult situations arise during the year, you can refer back to your notes and recall what you felt and experienced, or repeat one or some of the exercises.

Meditations

We hope your meditations will prove an invaluable tool on each of the Yuletide nights, each month, and whenever one of the twelve basic themes of the Yuletide nights touches or "speaks" to you.

To deepen and enrich your experience of each night's theme or topic, we have included an accompanying meditative introduction and meditation. They can be read out as guided meditations by a participant in a small group or recorded and played back for private use, such as via a suitable app on your cellphone. This can add an additional layer to your practice, but it is not absolutely essential to the work you do during the Nights of Yuletide. You can also use the meditations throughout the year. A different month is associated with each night/ each theme, so that you can refer back to any of the meditations to help in your self-discovery whenever you are affected by one of the twelve basic themes. We hope that you will have every opportunity to devote time to yourself during the Twelve Nights of Yuletide, and in the year that follows, and indeed throughout your whole life. We hope you will have time for yourself and to be yourself.

PART TWO

Themes and Time Qualities of the Twelve Nights of Yuletide

First Night of Yuletide

December 21/22
(St. Thomas' Night, winter solstice)

❖

Theme: Sense the quality of time
Assigned month: January

❖

Eternity is time
And time eternity –
Except when you yourself
Would make them different be.

Angelus Silesius
(German priest, translation Paul Carus)

A passage from the Christian Old Testament book Ecclesiastes,* often quoted but rarely heeded in daily life, begins with the words: "To every thing there is a season."

To every thing there is a season, and a time to every purpose under the heaven:
A time to be born, and a time to die; a time to plant, and a time to pluck up that
    which is planted;
A time to kill, and a time to heal; a time to break down, and a time to build up;
A time to weep, and a time to laugh; a time to mourn, and a time to dance;

---

* Ecclesiastes 3, King James Version

A time to cast away stones, and a time to gather stones together; a time to embrace,
    and a time to refrain from embracing;
A time to get, and a time to lose; a time to keep, and a time to cast away;
A time to rend, and a time to sew; a time to keep silence, and a time to speak;
A time to love, and a time to hate; a time of war, and a time of peace.
What profit hath he that worketh in that wherein he laboreth?
I have seen the travail, which God hath given to the sons of men to be exercised in it.
He hath made every thing beautiful in his time: also he hath set the world in their
    heart, so that no man can find out the work that God maketh from the
    beginning to the end.

In this passage, "time" does not refer to the time of day or time in the sense of an agenda. Instead, it is about the qualities of a particular time, of issues and undertakings for which the right time has come, for which the time is "ripe." It is about developing a feeling for precisely these things, sensing in our daily lives if the vibrations of time are auspicious for a particular undertaking, or, by the same token, if they are not.

People use various systems and tools to do this, such as horoscopes, divination cards, pendulums, or divining rods, but it is simpler to follow your intuition and rely on your feelings, your first impulse.

In each of the coming Nights of Yuletide, begin by practicing sensing or feeling the quality of the day and drawing conclusions about it. This is where your heart rather than your mind comes into play. Place your hands on your heart chakra and feel your energy, be aware of yourself, untouched for a moment by any tormenting thoughts and fears. Ask yourself questions and see how your heart responds, how you feel about them.

This rather unusual exercise will, of course, present its own challenges, especially in the busy holiday season, but it will help you to learn how to be sensitive to both yourself and the quality of time, even when under pressure.

As the passage points out, it is not limited to the qualities of a particular day but is primarily to do with periods or lengths of time, time "windows" that are favorable (or not, as the case may be) for particular undertakings. For example, does it feel as though something is "in the air"? Some form of movement? Or have things come to a halt? In the first instance, you should start setting things in motion, taking action; in the second, be patient and wait until the vibrations seem favorable for a new venture. If it is obviously not the right time, expect nothing for the moment. From now on, the daily themes will be an expression of a time quality, a time window in which you can focus on a topic or theme. There are also special time windows that relate to the broad life plan that you helped to shape before this incarnation began. Use this day and the Yuletide nights that follow to get a sense of whether you are on course. Whatever you wish for, whatever feels right, is allowed.

However, this exercise is not just for this particular day. It also applies to the days that follow and their different themes. We hope that getting the ball rolling on December 21 will make you more sensitive to the qualities of the period of time, of the space/time continuum of your life.

The passage in Ecclesiastes about the quality of time ends as follows:

I know that there is no good in them, but for a man to rejoice, and to do good in his life. And also that every man should eat and drink, and enjoy the good of all his labor, it is the gift of God.
I know that, whatsoever God doeth, it shall be for ever: nothing can be put to it, nor any thing taken from it: and God doeth it, that men should fear before him.
That which hath been is now; and that which is to be hath already been; and God requireth that which is past.

To be, to exist is to be in the present. The past may shape us and the future unsettle us or become a projection of our hopes and desires, but we only ever experience and enjoy Creation and life in the present, in being in the moment. There is no enjoyment in life without this relationship with the present, nor should the very brief time span of a moment stop us from experiencing it consciously. Everything that frightens or upsets us is an expression of a yesterday that has been constricted in our memories and in the self-imposed limits of our view of tomorrow.

Everything has its time, its season, in countless moments, including pleasure. Never let anyone take this from you; continue to take pleasure in things. Always be aware of the riches with which you have been blessed and the experience of divine love and power given to you, even when times seem dark. Do you accept all this? Unconditionally? Gifts are given to be used and enjoyed.

PRACTICES FOR THE FIRST YULETIDE NIGHT

Here we include practical advice with a choice of optional questions for your Yuletide journal.

LOOKING BACK ON JANUARY OF LAST YEAR

What were my experiences during the New Year celebrations?

How did I start the New Year?

What plans and resolutions did I make?

Were there any special celebrations (such as birthdays)?

Which people were especially important?

Did I go on any journeys?

What was particularly enjoyable?

Who gave me support?

What good things happened?

To whom or what should I offer thanks?

Did anything unpleasant happen?

Did I suffer any particular setbacks?

Were there any arguments, conflicts, disappointments?

Is there anyone I haven't yet forgiven?

Which situations or experiences during last January would I now like to cleanse or resolve?

How did I use my time over the past year?

Have I taken time for myself?

Was I in charge of my time?

Did I recognize time windows and make use of them?

REFLECTING ON THE THEME OF THE DAY

Sensing the quality of time

I place my hands on my heart chakra and sense my energy for a moment, feel myself, unencumbered by tormenting thoughts or fears. I ask myself some questions and feel the way my heart responds.

How does today feel for me?

If I acknowledge my feelings, how does that change my mood?

What feels good for me today?

How do I feel about all my plans for today, everything I want to do?

What should I do, but what do I actually feel like doing in reality?

What can I add or leave out to focus properly on the qualities of the day and enjoy them fully?

What have I always wanted to do and might it just match the qualities of this particular day?

Does my daily schedule feel good right now?

Please note that this exercise is generally recommended as a way of getting into the right frame of mind, the right mood for sensing the special quality of each Yuletide night.

Questions

My time

Who or what controls my time?

Is my time available to me?

How much time do I spend on what?

What is the rhythm of my day/my year?

Do I have time simply to be?

Do I take time for myself?

Do I allow time for myself?

How much time do I devote to my dreams and my goals?

Do I set myself conditions: I'll do this and that first, and then I'll have time?

Do I know how to recognize and interpret the signals that time sends?

My lifetime

Am I in the "right film" in my life?

Does my heart feel fulfilled with my current existence?

Does everything that is in my life now give me pleasure (people, relationships, activities, the general situation)?

What do I dream of?

What do I yearn for?

How does the difference between my dreams and reality feel?

Is it "time" for change?

Where should the journey of my life take me?

LOOKING AHEAD TO JANUARY IN THE COMING YEAR

Encounters and signs

What did I dream of today?

How was the weather, the general mood, the atmosphere?

What happened today?

Who or what did I encounter during my meditation (situations/individuals/animals/plants)?

What signs was I shown today?

How did "me time," the time for myself, feel today?

Did time drag or fly by?

Consciously shaping the future

What is my vision for this coming January?

What daydreams did I have today?

Did I have time for myself today? Was I able to consciously decide how I used my time?

What do I wish for in the coming year in terms of how I deal with my time every day?

What changes do I hope to make?

What time "windows" are coming up in this next year? What is on the horizon?

What decisions would I like to take?

A MEDITATION TO DEEPEN THIS EXPERIENCE

*Time to pause for breath, time for myself; the interval between
ending and beginning.*

Before something new can begin, what there was before must come to an end.

In general, we believe that the end of something simultaneously marks the start of something new.

However, what we almost never think about is that the beginning comes later.

There is a space between an end and a new beginning, an interval between something ending and something being imminent, something coming into being.

On this day, on every day in January, and whenever something old comes to an end, the space between ending and beginning will suddenly open up, and the gates of time will unlock.

Today is calling on you to stand still, to pause for a moment, and to be completely calm.

Fill this space of silence and emptiness, this place of power, creation, and creativity, with your love and your truth.

Use your breath to sense power flowing into you in this space with the following meditation.

MEDITATION

Make yourself comfortable.

Be aware of your body and how it feels.

Tense and relax your muscles, one by one.

Your feet, calf muscles, knees, and upper thighs.

Tense your buttocks and stomach muscles, your back and shoulders.

Tense your fingers, hands, arms, and neck muscles.

Pull a face (grimace) to tense the muscles of your head.

Fill your lungs with fresh oxygen.

Yawn and take a few deep breaths.

Collect your thoughts and be calm.

Breathe calmly, easily, and in your own rhythm.

Breathe deliberately and consciously as you strengthen the life force that flows through you and all living creatures.

Breathe from your diaphragm.

Breathe in and then out as if gently pressing the air against your pelvic floor.

Let it flow downward for a couple of seconds,

Raise your abdominal wall, gently curving it outward.

Now breathe in naturally and automatically.

Once you have raised your abdominal wall and the air has collected at the base of your lungs, hold your breath for around 4 seconds.

Now move the air up into your chest area to fill your lungs completely.

Raise your collarbones slightly to help and then breathe quickly down into your lungs.

Breathe in once more.

Breathe the air down, right to your pelvic floor.

Now slightly expand your abdominal wall and hold the air here to the count of 4: 1, 2, 3, 4.

Raise your collarbones slightly and let the air flow up through you. Breathe out.

Repeat this twice.

Can you feel the warmth that builds up when you hold the air in your belly?

It is the life force spreading through your body.

It is the gift of power given to you in the pause between inhaling and exhaling.

Now learn how to distribute this life force that you have gained through the simple action of breathing throughout your body.

Choose a part of your body that you would like to fill with this energy: perhaps your feet are cold.

When you breathe out this time, imagine that the energy is flowing directly into your feet.

Breathe in, breathe the air down, right to your pelvic floor.

Now slightly expand your abdominal wall and hold the air to the count of 4: 1, 2, 3, 4.

Lift your collarbones slightly and let the air flow up into your lungs.

Breathe out and empty your lungs.

Repeat this until you feel a stream of energy or increased warmth in the chosen part of your body.

Now take a few more breaths in the same way with a pleasant, easy rhythm.

I wish you strength in your life, in the moments that you consciously pause between breaths. On this Night of Yuletide and in the Nights of Yuletide to come, and ever after.

Second Night of Yuletide

December 22/23

⬥◦⬥

Theme: Find humility and devotion
Assigned month: February

⬥◦⬥

*Is humility this love, free of all judgment, rooted in awareness
of the cosmic order, that recognizes and accepts things the way that
they are, as they have to be?*

Theodor Fontane

Everything has its time and the time for everything will come; it will do so for you, too, as long as you are open and ready for it. Being ready to participate, to devote yourself to something, to say yes are all ways of describing the basic attitude that you can adopt in relation to today's time quality. Many people feel misunderstood and mistreated by all sorts of things. They rail against a fate they consider to be unfair. They are slow to accept personal responsibility for their current situation. They ask everyone for help but are unwilling to act on their own behalf, or at best do so only half-heartedly.

Humility has nothing to do with subservience or a lack of freedom, even if some definitions imply servile behavior. The Middle English word is derived from the Old French *humilité* and refers to the status of a servant, but in the religious sense it refers to the attitude of a person toward their Creator and accepting the circumstances of Creation.

The circumstances of Creation are immutable; there is no sense in rebelling against them or indeed any prospect of success. What would be the point? If the essence of Creation is to shape life from the power of love, then where lies the lack of liberty? Is (divine) love a limitation? Divine love even includes the human right to dissociate yourself from love; many people do this, either consciously or unconsciously. Love of Creation and of your neighbor requires you to love yourself, and this is precisely what many people seem to find not only difficult but often impossible or forbidden.

Humility is "being within love." This means to use the power of your heart to create and to shape. Practice this in the time quality of December 23. Do so with devotion, in other words, let yourself be "touched" inwardly by the task you have been given (or have given yourself). Devotion is loyalty given to God. Do not shoulder burdens that you cannot and do not wish to carry; do not take responsibility for things that are not your concern; do not try to police things over which you have no control. Give up what is not yours and ease your mind. Your heart will feel lighter, allowing you to develop a joy and passion for everything that is really within you. Devotion is the key to becoming who you really are.

PRACTICES FOR THE SECOND YULETIDE NIGHT

Here we include practical advice with a choice of optional questions for your Yuletide journal.

LOOKING BACK ON FEBRUARY OF LAST YEAR

Was I consciously aware of the days lengthening?
Were there any particular occasions to celebrate?
Which people were especially important to me?
Did I go on any journeys?
What was particularly enjoyable?

Who gave me support?

What good things happened to me?

For what and to whom should I be thankful?

Did anything unpleasant happen?

Did I suffer any particular setbacks?

Were there any arguments, conflicts, disappointments?

Is there anyone I haven't yet forgiven?

What situations and experiences during last February would I now like to cleanse or resolve?

On what occasions was I humble, practicing devotion and making the best of everything that happened to me?

When did I not manage to be humble and when did I rebel?

REFLECTING ON THE THEME OF THE DAY

Questions

Can I simply *be* or must I instead always be achieving something or providing some service in order to feel loved?

When and how often do I allow myself to simply *be*?

Do I need drama or emotional pain and suffering to feel like myself?

Do I feel in control of my life, of being self-reliant and making my own decisions?

Do I feel loved, that someone is with me and guiding me, or do I feel misunderstood or scorned, with someone blocking my path, bothering me, hemming me in?

What thing or person do I feel is to blame?

Do I feel trust in the world, in God, in the course my life is taking?

Do I feel "grounded," or would I like to get away, to escape?

How does it feel for me to let go, to "go with the flow" of life?

Do I have to control everything and know everything (in advance) or do I enjoy being surprised by life?

Affirmations

May your will and my will be one will.

It is divine will that I live out my uniqueness in my life, that I can feel my heart and be joyful, that I can dance and sing; that I simply am!

I will write my own affirmation on the subject of humility and devotion.

Exercise

Today, I will practice humility and consciously devote myself with all my heart to a particular situation, activity, task, creature, or person. What will that involve? How will it make me feel?

LOOKING AHEAD TO FEBRUARY IN THE COMING YEAR

Encounters and signs

What did I dream of today?

How was the weather today, the general mood, the atmosphere?

What happened today?

Who or what did I encounter during my meditation (situations/individuals/animals/plants)?

What signs was I shown?

How did I experience humility and devotion today?

Consciously shaping the future

What is my vision for this coming February?

What daydreams did I have today?

What do I wish for in the coming year with regard to how I approach humility and dedication?

To which people or life circumstances do I want to devote myself?

A MEDITATION TO DEEPEN THIS EXPERIENCE

I am saying yes. I am devoting myself to life.

Today, the door is open for you to consider to what or to whom you wish to devote yourself wholeheartedly and with enthusiasm.

Perhaps there are things you do every day that you do not really enjoy.

Perhaps you feel you were forced into your current job.

Today, on every day in February, and whenever you feel at odds with yourself or your destiny, the door is open for humility and devotion to life.

Today is calling on you to be still and pause for a moment, to say yes, and to wholly accept everything as it is now. In this spirit of consent and accord, fill this place of power, creativity, and action with your humility and devotion. Plant the seed of devotion in your life today. The following meditation will help.

MEDITATION

Make yourself comfortable.

Be aware of your body and how it feels.

Tense and relax your muscles, one by one.

First your feet, then your calf muscles, knees, and thighs.

Tense your buttocks, stomach muscles, back, and shoulders.

Tense your fingers, hands, arms, and neck.

Pull a face (grimace) to tense the muscles of your head.

Fill your lungs with fresh oxygen.

Yawn and take a few deep breaths.

Collect your thoughts and be calm.

Breathe calmly and easily, at your own rhythm.

What do you have planned for later?

What things do you "have" to do?

Choose one of today's tasks, perhaps one that you think will not be much fun, one that you may consider a "necessary evil" or that you simply do not like doing—a chore, an unpleasant obligation, or a challenge.

Choose one, whatever it might be.

When you have made your choice, place your left hand on your heart chakra, in the center of your chest.

Then place your right hand beneath it, at the top of your stomach, just below your ribcage, on your solar plexus.

Now focus your thoughts and feelings on the task selected for the exercise.

Devote your full attention to it with all your heart.

Hold it in your thoughts:

I am looking forward to this task; the outcome will be good for both myself and the task.

Think of the task with love:

I feel how this task will be achieved with love.

I accept it with love.

And with gratitude:

I am grateful for this opportunity,

I am grateful that I am healthy and able to do this task,

I am grateful that I am able to take action,

I am grateful for the experience that it will bring me.

Allow the energy to flow between your hands.

Notice how the energy changes as you devote yourself to the task with joy and love.

Allow this joy to flow through your body, spreading across it with every breath you take.

Feel your reservations and distaste dissolve in the face of this energy.

Relax the muscles of your face, allow yourself to smile or even laugh.

Now let this joy in your work radiate beyond your body into the world around you.

Fill your space, house, and the entire town with it, far out into the universe.

With all my heart, I wish for you to accept, in love and joy, all you are able do on this Yule night and in the Nights of Yuletide to come, and ever after.

Third Night of Yuletide

Theme: Discover the power of your heart
Assigned month: March

> As I began to love myself,
> I recognized that my mind can disturb me
> And it can make me sick.
> But as I connected it to my heart,
> My mind became a valuable ally.
> Today, I call this connection
> Wisdom of the Heart
>
> Extract from poem frequently
> attributed to Charlie Chaplin

Living life means taking action, action requires decisions, and having to make decisions often frightens us. We are frequently reluctant to make choices, but what happens if we choose not to decide, if we fail to exercise the power of free will? Something or someone else will do it for us and so become master of our fate. Viewed in this way, much of what happens to us is the result of a decision to remain passive. Hence, it is not really possible to choose to not decide, to make a "non-decision."

So make a decision with your heart and meet with it in a meditation.

Make yourself comfortable, either seated or lying down.

Starting with your feet, move all your limbs and muscles, consciously tensing each one briefly, including the muscles of your face.

Breathe in and fill your body with oxygen; yawn several times.

Breathe calmly and quietly, without trying to adopt any particular rhythm. If you are able to do so, try breathing from the abdomen (diaphragm).

Focus your attention on your feet. Imagine they are putting down roots in the earth, anchoring you to the ground. Breathe in the power of the earth through these roots, up into your legs and to your root chakra at the base of your spine. Allow its energy to rise up through your spine into your heart chakra.

Now focus your attention on your crown chakra and feel cosmic forces flowing into you, reaching down to your heart chakra.

Feel your heart chakra and sense the unifying power and influence of the energies of the Earth and the cosmos. You are a being of the Heavenly Father and the Earthly Mother. It is only here that you can feel this, where their impulses unite within you to give rise to your life.

Focus on the very core of your being. It is only here that you can know how your heart feels. Does it feel constrained or is it free and beating joyfully? Does the plan you have made feel good or like a burden?

When your head threatens to dominate your heart, or if you are feeling weighed down by your emotions, consciously return to the energy of your heart chakra once more and send it further into your body with every breath you take, until the love of your heart permeates your entire body.

Allow the power of your heart to shine more brightly than anything else, dissolving all the fears, cares, anxiety, rage, envy, and grief in its light, all the negative emotions that you are feeling.

Bathe your body in the fire of your heart; allow its power to inform your encounters with everyone and everything. Do this whenever you feel you have lost contact with your heart. One day you will realize that you have become one with it, you are your heart.

PRACTICES FOR THE THIRD YULETIDE NIGHT

Here we include practical advice with a choice of optional questions for your Yuletide journal.

LOOKING BACK ON MARCH OF LAST YEAR

Have I banished the phantoms of the dark season?

Did any form of cleansing take place, such as fasting or even cleaning the house?

Were there any particular occasions to celebrate?

Who were the people that were especially important to me?

Did I go on any journeys?

What was particularly enjoyable?

Who gave me support?

What good things happened?

For what or to whom am I thankful?

Did anything unpleasant happen?

Did I suffer any particular setbacks?

Were there any arguments, conflicts, disappointments?

Is there anyone I haven't yet forgiven?

What situations and experiences during last March would I now like to cleanse or resolve?

Was I able to "feel" my heart during the past year?

Did I follow it? Did I act according to my heart?

Did it "jump for joy," and if so when?

REFLECTING ON THE THEME OF THE DAY

Questions

How do I make decisions?

Do I follow my head, with a furrowed brow?

Or do I "follow my gut"? Are my fears and worries still in charge?

Do I know how it feels to act and speak from the heart, to listen to it and find answers there?

Meditation experience

I will focus on my heart space in the heart meditation (see page 54).

What did I encounter during the meditation? I will write down my experiences or use drawings or paintings to record them in images.

Exercise

Toward whom or what would I like to direct the full power of my heart today? It could be someone I love or someone that does not mean so much to me, it could be an animal, a plant, the natural world, Mother Earth, a natural being, or even an activity to which I devote myself fully, something that I do with heart and soul. I will write down my experiences or use drawings or paintings to sketch them out in images.

LOOKING AHEAD TO MARCH IN THE COMING YEAR

Encounters and signs

What daydreams did I have today?

What was the weather like? How was the general mood, the atmosphere?

What happened today?

Who or what did I encounter during my meditation (situations/individuals/animals/plants)?

What signs was I shown?

How did I experience the power of my heart today and what was I doing?

Consciously shaping the future

What is my vision for this coming March?

What daydreams did I have today?

What do I wish for the coming year in terms of how I handle my heart's strength?

What ideas, plans, people, activities, and decisions will make my heart feel as if it is bursting with joy?

A MEDITATION TO DEEPEN THIS EXPERIENCE

Feel the power of your heart.

Today, the door is open for you to bring the power of your heart into your life. Do you understand your heart? That small, quiet voice inside that is always there to deliver advice and support?

Do you know what your heart wants? What are your heartfelt desires?

Today, on any day in March, and whenever you are no longer sure of what your heart is trying to tell you, the door is open to connecting with it once more. Today is calling on you to stand still, to pause for a moment, and to listen carefully to your heart. How would you like to be heard?

Fill this space of silence and emptiness, this place of power, creation, and creativity with the strength of your heart. Feel the energy flowing into you in this space. Plant the seed to awaken the power of your heart within you today. The following meditation will assist you.

MEDITATION

Imagine you have tree-like roots at the soles of your feet.

Or perhaps they appear as roots of light.

Either way, you are a child of the Earth, and the Earth nourishes you through these roots, giving you all you need to live and taking away whatever has been consumed and used up, whatever is no longer needed.

Allow these roots to grow deep, pushing down further and further into the soil.

Now take in the power of the Earth through your roots.

Allow this power to rise with the rhythm of your breath, through your legs and up to the base of your spine.

Allow the power of the Earth to rise up through your energy channel to the center of your chest, to your heart chakra.

Now focus your attention on the very top of your head, where the powers of the universe flow down into your crown chakra.

Imagine receiving these powers, as the leaves in the tree canopy take up sunlight.

Let this power flow down from your crown, past your third eye, down through your throat, and into your heart chakra.

Now place one hand on top of the other in the center of your chest.

Immerse yourself in the place where the power of Heaven and Earth come together.

This is your heart, your center.

Feel your heart beating; let its glow radiate out.

Ask your heart to flood your whole body with its energy and light.

Fill your body with the light of your heart, with each breath, each heartbeat.

First your torso and then your arms and legs, and into your head.

Feel how your entire body begins to vibrate in the power of your heart, in the light of your soul, in the harmony between Heaven and Earth.

Bathe in the light of your heart on this Yule night, during the Nights of Yuletide to come, and ever after.

Fourth Night of Yuletide

December 24/25
(Christmas: Christmas Eve and Christmas Day)

———◆———

Theme: Find peace
Assigned month: April

———◆———

*If Christ were born
in Bethlehem a thousand times
and not in thee thyself;
then art thou lost eternally.*

Angelus Silesius
(translator unknown)

Christmas is also known as the "Feast of Love." We wish for peace as an essential expression of love, so the quality of the day and the traditions of the season go together well.

Peace is many things: self-assurance and self-knowledge, focusing on the core of our being, being in accord. It is when we make peace with ourselves, our fellow human beings, the natural world, and the universe. It is when we accept the path.

Peace is multifaceted and begins with each of us. Are you at peace and in harmony with yourself?

Besides "inner peace," peace is a social, even a universal duty that you can address and master as you follow your spiritual path. The writings of the Essenes can help us to gain an understanding of the dimensions of peace.

The Essenes formed a secret sect to practice and pass on the knowledge that was brought to Egypt after Atlantis sank into the ocean. The sect was founded around 6700 BCE, but it was not until around 111 CE that the last of their settlements (including Qumran on the Dead Sea, 1211 BCE) were wiped out under constant pressure from the Romans and Christianity. The Essenes preserved an esoteric tradition and offered spirited opposition to the repeated, and ultimately doomed, attempts to maintain the culture of Atlantis through the official priesthood and pharaohs. The Sevenfold Peace was at the core of their teachings.

Sevenfold Peace*

1. *Peace with the (material) body:*

   Our "solid" bodies are part of Mother Earth and the manifested matrix of our development in this incarnation. Here, the focus is on mastering the body, its health, and/or its recuperation through breathing.

2. *Peace with the mind:*

   We are the creators of the thoughts that determine our actions. The thinking body of an individual has a reciprocal relationship with the thinking body of the Earth and the cosmic ocean of thought (= perfection of the law). The aim is to act in harmony with the law as a prerequisite for healing all bodies (aura layers) of disharmony.

3. *Peace with the family:*

   The people in your environment, those closest to you whom you love. This refers not only to the family circle in the narrower sense, but also to all those who are close to us in life or during a period of our lives.

4. *Peace with humanity:*

   This includes social and economic peace, keeping chaotic circumstances at arm's length, and practicing a social system based on the laws of Nature and the cosmos, along with imparting ideas to the outside world (teaching, healing, helping).

---

*From *The Essene Gospel of Peace*, Book Three, *The Lost Scrolls of the Essene Brotherhood* by Dr. E. Bordeaux Székely, International Biogenic Society.

5. **Peace with culture:**

Engagement with great works of wisdom (cultivation of nature, scholarship, literature, art) as an expression of involvement with human creativity, positive influence on the vibrations of streams of thought (morphic resonance).

6. **Peace with the kingdom of the Earthly Mother:**

The foundation of human existence on the planet.

7. **Peace with the kingdom of the Heavenly Father:**

Inner, intuitive recognition of the Law as the sum of all love, all knowledge, and all power. Overcoming those limitations that we have imposed upon ourselves via our thinking centers, returning to God.

What does this Sevenfold Peace mean for us in concrete terms? The following questions will help to explain.

The body

Am I at peace with my body? Do I love and accept it as it is, or do I feel too fat, thin, unattractive, clumsy?

Affirmation: Today, I love and embrace my body. I thank it for making life possible for me, for functioning largely as it should, for being dependable and reminding me when I leave the path of love. I praise it, I can expect so much from it. It is resilient, resistant, and strong, and yet also sensitive and gentle. It brings me much pleasure and makes it possible for me to be here, to live in the material world. I love my body.

The mind

Am I at peace with my mind, my thoughts? Do I have control over them, or do my thoughts take on an independent existence? Do I allow them to work against me, against my heart, against everything that is going well for me in life?

Affirmation: I am the master of my thoughts. When I listen to my heart, my thoughts give way to its desires. Today, I will rein in my thoughts and not let them get out of hand. I will calm and quieten my thoughts.

Family

Am I at peace with my family, with my parents, children, partner, and relatives; with my chosen family, my colleagues, my friends?

Ritual: I will begin my day by sending good wishes and positive thoughts to those to whom, deep down, I feel really close at this stage in my life. I visualize this group of people, starting with those in my immediate circle (children, partner), moving on to my parents and friends, and then to my colleagues. I send out energy to them as a group or individually, one at a time, adding my best wishes for the day or the week, or for a particular undertaking or event. If I happen to have a problem with one of these people, I will make energetic contact with them and in my thoughts explain to them how I feel, even if it is anger or grief. I will forgive them and ask in turn for forgiveness and understanding. If I recall an unpleasant situation in this context, I will send energy into the space-time of this experience and request that it may be good for all those involved.

Humanity

Am I at peace with the people I meet outside, in the street, in shops, on public transport, in traffic? Am I at peace with the people I talk to on the phone or encounter in my professional life?

Affirmation: I forgive myself for those times when I was unfriendly, rude, or dismissive to other people. May they forgive me. I undertake not to react hastily or irritably today if confrontation or friction should arise. I will take a deep breath, using my breathing to dissolve unpleasant feelings. I will stay calm but will express my wishes or reasons for being upset clearly.

Culture

Am I at peace with my surroundings? Am I at peace with my apartment and its contents, with my clothes, with the place and environment in which I live and with the buildings and the world around me?

Ritual: I use my feelings to explore the key places around me: my living, sleeping, and working areas, my garden and favorite walks, and so on. I reconcile myself with the objects, spaces, circumstances, and places that I cannot change. I distance myself from the things I do not need and that are not good for me. If something cannot be changed, whether an object or a particular space, I will direct three or four minutes' energy toward it and simply reflect on it, but without intention.

The Earthly Mother

Am I at peace with Mother Earth and her beings, the natural world? Do I respect and appreciate the nourishment and raw materials that the Earth provides?

Prayer*

Mother Earth and I are one.
She gives my body nourishment for life.
The strength of the soil
flows through my body, giving life.
The sun provides the fire of life.
Water makes my blood flow.
The air helps me breathe the current of life.
I take delight in the interplay of the elements.
They bring strength and beauty to everything
under the sun.

The Heavenly Father

Am I at peace with the Heavenly Father, the spiritual world, and its beings? Do I trust that they will guide me to what is best for me, that everything that happens is good, that I am loved and never forgotten? Or do I rail against the workings of the Creator by not appreciating myself, by failing to believe and put trust in myself, and thus in Him as my Creator? Can I accept my path, my destiny, without reservation, or do I constantly feel torn this way and that?

---

* Phrasing taken from the Essene communion

Prayer*
The Heavenly Father and I are one.
He gave me eternal life and
my creative powers.
May they bring joy and plenty
to me as well as to those around me,
and may His will guide my deeds.
May His love cleanse my emotional body
and His wisdom illuminate my thoughts.
Peace be with me and on Earth.

_____
* Phrasing taken from the Essene communion

PRACTICES FOR THE FOURTH YULETIDE NIGHT

Here we include practical advice with a choice of optional questions for your Yuletide journal.

LOOKING BACK ON APRIL OF LAST YEAR

How did I experience the changeable month of April?

Were there any special celebrations?

Which people were especially important to me?

Did I go on any journeys?

What was particularly pleasant?

Who gave me support?

What good things happened?

To what or to whom should I offer thanks?

Did anything unpleasant happen?

Did I suffer any particular setbacks?

Were there any arguments, conflicts, disappointments?

Is there anyone I haven't yet forgiven?

What situations and experiences during last April would I now like to cleanse or resolve?

What was I at peace with last year?

When was there discord instead of peace?

In what aspect of life am I already close to achieving peace?

REFLECTING ON THE THEME OF THE DAY

Exercise

I will select one of the aspects of the Sevenfold Peace (peace with my body, mind, and family; with humanity and culture; with the Earthly Mother and the Heavenly Father) where I sense there is the greatest lack in my life. I will choose appropriate affirmations, prayers, and exercises, or write my own affirmations and work with them today.

I will choose the aspect for which I sense the greatest level of peace and celebrate it today, giving special thanks for the peace granted to me.

How will I celebrate? How will I express my thanks and joy?

What does a fulfilling celebration involve for me?

LOOKING AHEAD TO APRIL IN THE COMING YEAR

Encounters and signs

What did I dream of today?

How was the weather, the general mood, the atmosphere?

What happened today?

Who or what did I encounter during my meditation (situations/people/animals/plants)?

What signs was I shown?

What gifts did I give today? What messages did I send with them?

What gifts did I receive today? What messages did they bring me?

How did I experience peace? What was I doing?

Which of the different aspects of the Sevenfold Peace did I experience today in particular?

Consciously shaping the future

What is my vision for this coming April?

What were my daydreams about today?

What do I wish for the coming year in terms of how I approach peace, and peace in relation to my body and my mind, my family, humanity, culture, Mother Earth and the Heavenly Father?

What kind of peace would I like to devote myself to in particular?

A MEDITATION TO DEEPEN THIS EXPERIENCE

Peace begins with me.

The gates of time are open for you to make peace part of your life. Have you ever wondered if there is a connection between your experience of peace and the peace in your immediate surroundings, or farther out in the world? There is indeed a link, as we are ultimately all interconnected with one another.

Are you at peace with your family, your friends, and with your immediate surroundings? You will not find peace on the outside, nor will you find it in the ideal partner, perfect children, or in the admiration of work colleagues. Your family and friends cannot give you inner peace.

Today, on every day in April, and whenever you feel the absence of peace within you or others, the door is open to put an end to this inner conflict and to make peace.

Today is calling on you to stand still, pause for a moment, and make perfect peace with yourself. Fill this space of silence and emptiness, this place of power, creation, and creativity with your peace.

MEDITATION

Make yourself comfortable.

Be aware of your body and how it feels.

Tense and relax your muscles, one at a time.

First your feet, then calf muscles, knees, and thighs.

Tense your buttocks, stomach muscles, back, and shoulders.

Tense your fingers, hands, arms, and neck.

Pull a face (grimace) to tense the muscles of your head.

Fill your lungs with fresh oxygen.

Yawn and take a few deep breaths.

Now collect your thoughts and be calm.

Breathe calmly, easily, and in your own rhythm.

Place your right hand on your stomach, just below your navel.

Place your left hand on your heart chakra, in the center of your chest.

Feel your heart beneath your left hand.

Is it calm? Do you feel composed?

Is your heart beating with a gentle and regular rhythm?

Be fully aware for a moment of allowing the healing energy of your hand to flow into your heart chakra.

Breathe quietly and evenly.

Take a brief pause, then focus on your right hand lying on your stomach.

Does your stomach feel warm?

Is it quiet and calm?

Take a moment to allow healing energy to flow into your stomach from your right hand.

Now picture your two hands forming a bridge of energy across your body.

Ask for your heart and stomach to be brought into harmony across this bridge.

Feel how your heart loves you, and gently transfer this vibration of peace through your right hand into your abdomen.

Allow the thoughts and feelings now rising up to simply flow away. Pass no judgment on them.

Now turn your attention to your heart and guide its light back to your abdomen.

Allow any feelings that are troubling you to bathe in this light.

The light of your heart is love, and wherever love shines out, there is peace both within you and all around you.

Hence humanity's ancient greeting:

Peace be with you! Peace be with you!

May peace be with you on this Yule night, in the Nights of Yule to come, and ever after.

Fifth Night of Yuletide

December 25/26
(Christmas Day and Boxing Day/St. Stephen's Day)

Theme: Embrace trust
Assigned month: May

As soon as you trust yourself, you will know how to live.

Johann Wolfgang von Goethe

The word "trust" is linked linguistically to the word group related to "true," deriving from the Old Norse *traustr*, meaning strong and solid. Strength and solidity are expressions of trust, in the rightness and truth of a belief or a conviction, for example. If this trust is in your own abilities or potential, it is termed self-confidence. It is a reciprocal relationship. If you have no confidence in yourself, you will have no trust in other people or things; you will not engage with life or explore your particular strengths and abilities, which you will eventually lose.

Trust is based on self-knowledge and self-confidence, on the certainty that the all-encompassing peace of the heart will support us in life and allow us to face and help shape its challenges.

Our souls are part of the divine energy; with our divine core we are of God and His fire nourishes us from the energy of our souls. At the same time, we are children of an Earth that gives us our bodies and provides us with nourishment. The energies of both come together and combine in our heart chakras. It is only there that we feel our own true selves, untrammeled by emotions or thoughts.

Practice trusting in the certainty that this Earth loves you and nourishes you, that you can return to the cradle of Mother Earth and surrender to the guidance of the Heavenly Father.

Perform a meditation. Visualize a tree, just as the Essenes did. Be this tree. Use your roots to take in the power of the Earth, use your branches to absorb the energies of the universe. Allow the interplay of the powers of Creation to flood through you and support you.

If everything is of God and comes from God, and if we also bear a divine core within us, it follows there is no difference between trusting in ourselves and trusting in God.

If our body is formed from the dust of the Earth and the Earth nourishes us, then there is no difference between trusting in ourselves and being grounded, trusting in the Earth.

PRACTICES FOR THE FIFTH YULETIDE NIGHT

Here we include practical advice with a choice of optional questions for your Yuletide journal.

LOOKING BACK ON MAY OF LAST YEAR

Was I able to experience and celebrate the beginning of spring?

Were there any special festivities?

Which people were especially important to me?

Did I go on any journeys?

What was particularly nice?

Who gave me support?

What good things happened?

To what or whom should I offer thanks?

Did anything unpleasant happen?

Did I suffer any particular setbacks?

Were there any arguments, conflicts, disappointments?

Is there anyone I haven't yet forgiven?

What situations and experiences during last May would I now like to cleanse or resolve?

Did I trust myself, did I trust life?

Who else did I trust in my family or at work?

In what circumstances do I find it difficult to trust?

Who or what did I fail to trust?

Who betrayed my trust?

REFLECTING ON THE THEME OF THE DAY

Affirmations

I have trust in God and divine guidance. I have trust in myself, in my gifts and my strengths. I have trust in my family and in people. I meet people and encounter circumstances that are "just right" for a particular situation; I can learn from them and they can help me. I am always in the right place at the right time.

I enjoy the natural world and trust in the interplay of the elements. The Earth is a hospitable place for me, a home. I trust in the forces of Nature. I live in the trust that I am safe and protected.

I will develop my own affirmations for those aspects of life where I always find it difficult to trust and have frequent doubts.

Exercise

I will choose one or two aspects of life that present me with particular challenges with regard to trust, and will then think about the times that things turned out well, despite my fears and doubts. I will reconnect with these situations and the vibrations emanating from the trust they radiate. I will try to pay more attention to the things that promote my trust in being here, in the moment, however insignificant they may appear, and dispel any feelings of distrust.

LOOKING AHEAD TO MAY IN THE COMING YEAR

Encounters and signs

What did I dream of today?

How was the weather, the general mood, the atmosphere?

What happened today?

Who or what did I encounter during my meditation (situations/individuals/animals/plants)?

What signs was I shown?

Who placed trust in me today?

Consciously shaping the future

What is my vision for this coming month of May?

What daydreams did I have today?

In whom or in what have I consciously placed my trust today?

In whom or in what would I like to place special trust in the year to come?

What are my ambitions for change in terms of trust?

A MEDITATION TO DEEPEN THIS EXPERIENCE

I have trust. The peace in my heart will support me.
You too can have perfect trust—in yourself, in your fellow human
beings, in your life.

Can you recall a situation where you had complete trust? Do you have it now? There are times in our lives when everything seems to come together and make sense. It could be something as simple as sitting by the sea and hearing the waves pounding on the shore or feeling love and affection for someone. In moments like these, it feels as if we share a connection with all things and we have complete trust; we feel pure happiness. From now on, you will be able to access this feeling for yourself. Today, on every day in May, and whenever you lose faith in yourself, in life or in other people, the door will be wide open to total trust.

Today is calling on you to stand still, pause for a moment, and trust completely. Fill this space of silence and emptiness, this place of power, creation, and creativity, with your trust.

Plant the seed of trust today. Sow this seed with the following meditation.

MEDITATION

Make yourself comfortable.

Be aware of your body and how it feels.

Tense and relax your muscles, one by one.

First your feet, calf muscles, knees, and thighs.

Tense your buttocks, stomach muscles, back, and shoulders.

Tense your fingers, hands, arms, and neck.

Pull a face (grimace) to tense the muscles of your head.

Fill your lungs with fresh oxygen.

Yawn and take a few deep breaths.

Now collect your thoughts and be calm.

Breathe evenly, in your own rhythm.

Relax, breathe quietly and softly, and focus on your feelings.

Can you think of a situation when you felt deep trust?

Think of a time when you were absolutely certain that everything was okay.

Think of a time when you felt totally safe.

Focus on this time in your thoughts.

Recall whether you were alone or among a group of people.

An image from your childhood may come to you, and even if it is a little hazy, do you feel protected?

Is that what is in your mind? Can you feel it?

If so, concentrate harder and go deeper in your mind into that place or situation, whatever it was like: with people, animals, or in nature.

You will experience it all, now, in this very moment.

Open your heart and immerse yourself in the emotions of the situation.

Make this moment the present and return to the here and now.

Stay firmly in tune with these feelings.

Keep this memory alive within you and call it to mind whenever your trust begins to waver.

Recall these feelings whenever you need to and you will soon connect with trust in this moment.

May you have a perfect connection with trust in the here and now, on this Yule night, in the Nights of Yule to come, and ever after.

Sixth Night of Yuletide

December 26/27

◈—◈—◈

Theme: Discover tranquility
Assigned month: June

◈—◈—◈

Whatever is done with no pauses will not last.

Ovid

When we are at rest, we are not active. We may make the conscious decision to go to sleep (the biological state of rest), but the act of sleep itself is not conscious. People might disturb us, by creating noise, for example, and we may not be able to find rest when we are not at peace with ourselves. Being at peace is a state or condition, a gift. Finding rest and tranquility is something we may achieve before we go to our "final rest." The world outside may be able to help us find peace of mind, but there is no guarantee, even if we spend time in the most peaceful of locations.

Self-assurance and self-confidence are milestones on the path to inner peace—tranquility.

Allow yourself to *be*. We do not have to reach a particular level of achievement to love ourselves and to gain the love of God. All we need is self-assurance, a calmness within ourselves as we go about our everyday lives, a sense that we can live according to our own rhythm, despite anything that may intrude and disturb us.

A feeling of tranquility does not indicate a lack of involvement or being disengaged from society. Indeed, it is quite the opposite: it is a precondition for being creatively involved in our community. If you feel slightly unsettled, a certain creative unease within you, it is not necessarily a bad thing, as long as it derives from an enjoyment of being involved, of engaging with people and projects. Do not let yourself be driven by others, never let yourself feel "railroaded" into something. Do not allow yourself to constantly feel dissatisfied and do not judge or condemn yourself. Set yourself goals that are achievable at your own pace.

Always remember: you do not "have to" do anything. No one has the right to demand something from you, nor should you demand it from yourself. May tranquility be the source from which you can draw inspiration.

The Source

Movement only
In the sediment,
Like sand, grain by grain.
No eddies lift
The floral
Membrane
Of heart-like
Peace.

And yet,
Behind the
Band of reeds,
There ripples
Across the turf
The power that wells up
From tranquility.

Werner Hartung

PRACTICES FOR THE SIXTH YULETIDE NIGHT

Here we include practical advice with a choice of optional questions for your Yuletide journal.

LOOKING BACK ON JUNE OF LAST YEAR

What was my experience of the early part of summer?

Were there any particular celebrations?

Who were the people who were especially important to me?

Did I go on any journeys?

What was particularly enjoyable?

Who gave me support?

What good things happened?

To what or to whom should I offer thanks?

Did anything unpleasant happen?

Did I suffer any particular setbacks?

Were there any arguments, conflicts, disappointments?

Is there anyone I haven't yet forgiven?

What situations and experiences during last June would I now like to cleanse or resolve?

Who or what prevented me from finding tranquility in the past year?

When did I find pleasant moments of peace?

REFLECTING ON THE THEME OF THE DAY

A meditation for creating silence

For many people the Holy Grail of a peaceful environment is impossible to find, but with a little practice I do now manage to "switch off." But how much better it would be if I did not feel as though the various disruptive sounds and commotion coming at me from outside were targeting me, but instead could just see them as the normal "background noise" of everyday life.

I will begin this meditation as I do for the heart (see page 54). Once I have made a connection, I will listen attentively and focus fully on all the sounds around me. This time, however, I will not try to ignore them and will make no judgments.

I begin with the sounds that I can hear from outside, such as traffic passing in the street, children playing, people arguing, birds singing, planes flying overhead, or an ambulance passing with blaring sirens. I then concentrate on the sounds within my building, in other rooms or apartments. I notice everything passively, even if it is my own children being noisy or playing music at full volume. Now I focus on the sounds in the meditation room—a clock ticking, the floor creaking, a fly buzzing.

Next, I switch off even this level in my consciousness and become fully alert to the sounds of my body—my heart beating, my pulse thudding, my stomach rumbling. I am also aware of my body's involuntary movements, such as muscles twitching. Things that would normally disturb or even annoy me become the object of my meditation. I make peace with them; they are part of my surroundings, part of me, of myself. I simply allow them to *be* and I notice that they also let me *be*. They allow me to be in the peace that I desire.

If you find that this meditation is not entirely successful the first time you attempt it, be reassured that it will gradually improve with practice. After all, you are trying to creating calm for yourself in an environment that may be anything but calm.

LOOKING AHEAD TO JUNE IN THE COMING YEAR

Encounters and signs

What did I dream of today?

How was the weather, the general mood, the atmosphere?

What happened today?

Who or what did I encounter during my meditation (situations/individuals/animals/plants)?

What signs was I shown?

What sounds did I hear today?

Was I able to be calm?

How did that feel?

What caused that sense of calm?

Consciously shaping the future

What is my vision for this coming June?

What daydreams did I have today?

Which sounds did I consciously notice during the meditation?

Where or in what would I like to find peace in the coming year?

A MEDITATION TO DEEPEN THIS EXPERIENCE

I will find tranquility, even if there is none in my immediate surroundings.

Today is about discovering tranquility. Are you always busy and stressed? Contemporary society seems to be involved in some kind of competition (the winner is generally the most stressed person!), with the ability to find peace now a rare and precious gift. However, this train of thought can in itself lead to the frantic existence that we all seem to live. I want to help you find tranquility right now, even if there is precious little peace and quiet around you.

Today, on every day in June, and whenever you are stressed and restless, or cannot find peace around you, the door is open to finding complete calm.

Today is calling on you to stand still, pause for a moment, and be completely at peace. Fill this space of silence and emptiness, this place of power, creation, and creativity, with your calm.

The following meditation invites you to awaken the gift of discovering peace within you, and to sow this seed today.

MEDITATION

Listen carefully to the sounds that you can hear.

Focus on the sounds closest to you, in your immediate environment.

What do you hear in your home?

Can you hear footsteps?

Are noises coming from the kitchen, from appliances?

From the refrigerator or the washing machine?

Listen carefully to the sounds reaching you from outside.

Hear the neighbors, sounds from the street, loud music, joyful laughter, shouts, birdsong, a crying child, traffic, or a siren.

Yes, people are going about their everyday business, but does that really affect you?

Life is noisy, everywhere. Even in the mountains you will still hear the sound of a waterfall.

You too are "working," your body is functioning.

Perhaps you can feel a muscle twitching?

Or a twinge of pain or an itch?

Can you hear the blood pulsing in your veins?

Your breath?

All living things have an effect on our senses.

Everything you hear is an expression of life.

Life does not disturb, it just *is*.

Be in accord, be at peace, with everything that is within you.

Be in accord, be at peace, with everything that is around you.

Notice but do not judge.

Be part of this life.

Take part, not apart from life but as a part of it.

In this moment, focus your attention on yourself and your heart once more.

Step out of time for a moment, out of what surrounds you.

Allow tranquility to enter your mind.

I wish you tranquility on this Yule night, in the Nights of Yuletide to come, and ever after.

Seventh Night of Yuletide

December 27/28

Theme: Self-care
Assigned month: July

The highest good is the harmony of the soul with itself.

Seneca

The theme for December 24 is learning to love yourself and being in harmony and at peace with yourself. If you turn the concept of loving your neighbor as you love yourself around, it gives rise to a question: How can you give to others something that you deny yourself? Genuine love of your neighbor is predicated on love of yourself. In this respect, loving yourself is entirely acceptable and indeed virtually a precondition. It is not a mark of selfishness, nor even "healthy" selfishness; you do not have to apologize for love or for loving yourself.

Think about your average day: Do you spend it taking care of people? Do you make enough time for yourself, taking into account that you may have children or a partner to look after?

By the same token, are you happy to take or accept something from others without considering whether you could have dealt with it yourself alone? Do you have the desire and the energy to do something yourself? You cannot expect your neighbor to give you what only you can give yourself. In this sense, be gentle with yourself, treat yourself to something nice, spoil yourself. Think about your desires, wishes, and dreams; discover your fantasies, visions, and ideas. You have earned the right for things to go well. Focus on what excites and interests you and you will find the energy to achieve your desires.

PRACTICES FOR THE SEVENTH YULETIDE NIGHT

Here we include practical advice with a choice of optional questions for your Yuletide journal.

LOOKING BACK ON JULY OF LAST YEAR

Last summer, did I enjoy the month of July?
Were there any celebrations?
Which people were especially important to me?
Did I go on any journeys?
What was particularly pleasant?
Who gave me support?
What good things happened?
To whom or for what should I be thankful?

Did anything unpleasant happen?
Did I suffer any particular setbacks?

Were there any arguments, conflicts, disappointments?

Is there anyone I have yet to forgive?

What situations and experiences during last July would I now like to cleanse or resolve?

Which people or things did I look after rather than taking care of myself?

REFLECTING ON THE THEME OF THE DAY

Reflections

In which areas of life do I look after myself and take responsibility, while also taking things easy?

Do I assume material and financial responsibility for my life?

Do I take responsibility for my feelings and my well-being?

Do I allow myself the luxury of dressing nicely, living comfortably, doing a fulfilling job, eating well and healthily, taking exercise, finding peace of mind, while also having fun and enjoying life?

I will note in which respects I do take good care of myself, but also where I could do better and spoil myself more.

Exercise

Today, I will stop worrying about other people and release myself from any obligations to them. Instead, I will listen to my heart. I may discover just what a challenge this can be and how taking care of others is in fact much easier. Today, I will practice being really attentive to my heart. I will follow its desires, go with the flow, and see what life has in store for me.

I will record the gifts that life gives me along the way in my journal, making notes or using photos or sketches.

If my day has already been planned, I will carry out this exercise in my imagination and start right away. I will imagine that I have a day free to do exactly as I like, however improbable this may seem at the moment. I will plan to do exactly what I want, even if it is only in my head or on paper for now. And since thoughts and words precede action, I will make a written note of what I want to do or sketch it out in my journal; after all, to take delivery of something you must first place your order!

LOOKING AHEAD TO JULY IN THE COMING YEAR

Encounters and signs

What did I dream of today?

How was the weather, the general mood, the atmosphere?

What happened today?

Who or what did I encounter during my meditation (situations/individuals/animals/plants)?

What signs was I shown today?

What signs did I receive about those aspects of my life in which I could take more care of myself?

How did it feel to be gentler with myself?

Consciously shaping the future

What is my vision for this coming July?

What daydreams did I have today?

In which areas of life would I like to take better care of myself during the year to come: financial independence, a fulfilling job, a comfortable home, a healthy diet, nice clothes, regular exercise, feelings of calm, joy, and serenity? And how can I achieve these things?

A MEDITATION TO DEEPEN THIS EXPERIENCE

I take care of myself because I love myself.

Today, the door is open to thinking about taking care of yourself. But what does this actually mean? It is just another way of saying that you love yourself; the more self-love you allow yourself, the more love you will radiate in the world, and the more likely you are to attract positive people and situations into your life.

On this day, on every day in July, and whenever you feel worthless or dependent on other people, the door is open for you to decide to take care of yourself.

Today is calling on you to stand still, pause for a moment, and love yourself completely. Fill this space of silence and emptiness, this place of power, creation, and creativity, with your self-love and your sense of personal responsibility. Today is the day to awaken the self-love and personal responsibility in your life, to plant the seed of self-love within it. Take part in an encounter with yourself in the following meditation.

MEDITATION

Take a deep breath in and out.

Close your eyes.

You are outdoors, in the open air.

A wonderful summer's day dawns around you.

The early morning mist has burned off and a gentle dew remains on the grass.

You breathe in the scent of the flowers, the fresh meadows, and the fields.

The sun rises above the treetops of the small copse

toward which you are slowly strolling.

Its rays lift your heart.

Once you have reached the tree line,

you leave the fields and meadows behind you.

Full of curiosity, yet hesitating slightly, you follow a path

never seen before.

It leads to the small woodland copse.

As you walk, you listen to the song with which the bird kingdom

greets you and the day.

When a clearing suddenly opens up in front of you,

you stop and stand still in surprise.

In the center of the clearing, you see yourself.

You see yourself,

sitting on the soft moss in the clearing.

You watch yourself bathing in the sun's rays

as they gently filter through the canopy of leaves to caress your
skin.

You see yourself breathing in the fragrance of the forest
around you.

You watch as you eat sweet berries.

You see how you observe the world around you with love.

You see how you are in perfect harmony with yourself.

Joy and deep love flood through you,
love of yourself.

Suddenly, you, the *you* in the center of the clearing,

looks up at you, the observer.

Your eyes meet.

And suddenly you know

that you have been waiting here for yourself forever.

You approach each other, slowly at first but then more quickly.

Once you reach each other,

you fall into each other's arms

in a loving embrace.

You absorb all the happiness,

all the harmony within you,

in a loving embrace,

melting into your light self

until finally you stand alone but not lonely

in the center of the clearing,

filled with love for yourself.

Enjoy this wonderful feeling for a few more moments,

and slowly return to the reality of this day.

Remain immersed in the mood of the sunlit morning

on which you encountered yourself in love.

I wish you self-love, for yourself, on this Yule night, in the Nights
of Yule to come, and ever after.

Eighth Night of Yuletide

December 28/29

❖

Theme: Truth and clarity
Assigned month: August

❖

Clarity is not a matter of form, but of love.

Leo Tolstoy

To fully understand another person, the person you wish to understand should on occasion be you. Those who know what a thought system is will applaud me.

This insight comes from the writings of the German philosopher and physicist Georg Christoph Lichtenberg (1742–99). It illustrates just how hard it is to communicate truths and realities and, importantly, to be aware of your own "truth."

Our universe may function according to apparently immutable laws that we recognize as truth or reality, but even our physics-based and technology-dependent view of the world is constantly changing. We are left with models created by humans, representations of what actually exists. In this respect, it is difficult (perhaps not essential, but even impossible) to construct an image of the Creator and his Creation. From this perspective, there are realities, but not *one* reality, truths, but not *the* truth.

If there is a general law, namely that of love, then it also includes your right to create and live your own reality. Truth is therefore always *your* truth, *your* take on reality; truth is *your* model, *your* plan, *your* actions. It is what originates from and corresponds to the promptings of your heart. However, it requires clarity, and, most importantly, the clarity to see things clearly from your own perspective, from the point of view of self-love, free from fear, illusions, or external precepts.

The corollary of your basic existential right also holds true, as follows:

Truth will only become reality when you recognize things clearly and act in clarity; love is only found where clarity prevails, where you are clear about your goals and path.

Clarity, when revealed, may well shock or disenchant, but it is nevertheless an asset. When you finally find the courage to articulate it and bring things out into the open, it may initially have a disturbing effect on the people around you. Think about the likely consequences of your truth for yourself and for others. What do you want to change and when? Who should you talk to? What should you do to achieve clarity in your own issues?

PRACTICES FOR THE EIGHTH YULETIDE NIGHT

Here we include practical advice, with a choice of optional questions for your Yuletide journal.

LOOKING BACK ON AUGUST OF LAST YEAR

Was I able to take a holiday last August?
What special celebrations took place?
Which people were especially important to me?
Did I go on any journeys?
What was particularly pleasant?

Who gave me support?

What good things happened?

To whom or what should I offer thanks?

Did anything unpleasant happen?

Did I suffer any particular setbacks?

Were there any arguments, conflicts, disappointments?

Is there anyone I haven't yet forgiven?

What situations and experiences that occurred during last August would I now like to cleanse or resolve?

In which areas of my life was there a lack of clarity?

To whom did I not express myself clearly in the last year?

REFLECTING ON THE THEME OF THE DAY

Exercise

I will enter a peaceful place, a relaxed and meditative state; I will be there for myself. I will call to mind the insights, feelings, and discoveries of the past days and ask myself questions.

What is my truth?

Do I know my truth?

Can I bear to look my truth in the face?

Do I act according to my truth, my principles?

What fears and precepts determine my life and actions, either consciously or (until now) unconsciously, preventing me from recognizing my truth?

What must I add to or remove from my life in order to become closer to my truth?

Am I clear about things?

Is there clarity in my thoughts, words, and deeds?

What fears and precepts determine my life and actions, either consciously or (until now) unconsciously, preventing me from bringing clarity into my life?

To whom do I not want to be clear with truth? To whom am I pretending?

Who can I approach with clarity and truth?

What do I want to express and to whom in order to achieve clarity?

LOOKING AHEAD TO AUGUST IN THE COMING YEAR

Encounters and signs

What did I dream of today?

How was the weather, the general mood, the atmosphere?

What happened today?

Who or what did I encounter during my meditation (situations/individuals/animals/plants)?

What signs was I shown?

What felt true to me today?

What appeared clear to me?

Consciously shaping the future

What is my vision for this coming August?

What daydreams did I have today?

In what area of my life would I like to have more clarity during the year to come?

A MEDITATION TO DEEPEN THIS EXPERIENCE

With hand on heart, I profess its truth.

Today, the door is open to thinking about truth and clarity. Be clear about the fact that there are realities, but no single, exclusive reality. There are truths, but no single, exclusive truth.

There are many truths and many realities. Take maps, for example: numerous maps may be made of a particular city, but the maps are not the city itself. The same applies to our reality and our truth: each of us has our own truth, our own reality. We have a tendency to regard our own truth and our own reality as *the* truth and *the* reality, when we have really only created them ourselves from images. These images are not reality itself, nor are they truth itself. Truths and realities are complex and multilayered.

Today, on every day in August, and whenever you have become entangled in untruths or lies, the door is open to declare your truth with clarity.

The following meditation will help you to awaken your truth, your genuine expression in life. Plant the seed of clarity and truth in your life today. Truth needs clarity. Your truth is truly already present and you will find it within yourself, within your heart. Your heart always knows what is true for you, and today you will find it easy to achieve ultimate clarity.

MEDITATION

Make yourself comfortable.

Be aware of your body and how it feels.

Tense and relax your muscles, one at a time.

First your feet, calf muscles, knees, and thighs.

Tense your buttocks, stomach muscles, back, and shoulders.

Tense your fingers, hands, arms, and neck.

Pull a face (grimace) to tense the muscles of your head.

Fill your lungs with fresh oxygen.

Yawn and take a few deep breaths.

Now collect your thoughts and be still.

Breathe calmly, easily, and in your own rhythm.

Relax and take some soft, gentle breaths.

Do you already have a particular "lie" or truth in mind?

A truth you are still not wholly sure is your truth?

Do you still lack certainty and clarity?

Choose an issue about which you are still not clear and for which there may be two conflicting solutions.

Perhaps a realization or insight that is slowly dawning on you, an idea, or a plan.

Relax and place both hands on your heart chakra in the center of your chest.

Be aware that it is here that your soul always speaks to you, in the place where the forces of the universe and of the Earth meet and unite.

It is here that you feel your truth and find clarity.

That is why we say "hand on heart" in situations where there are two answers or options.

Choose one and focus on how your heart feels.

Does it feel open and receptive?

Or does it feel confined and restricted?

The answer now lies in your heart.

It does not lie in your head or your gut.

What is your heart saying?

If there is a second possible solution, repeat the exercise.

Make another connection with your heart, the source of your soul energy.

Focus on how it is feeling.

Is your heart open and receptive?

Or does it feel confined and restricted?

How does the alternative option feel in the light of your heart?

Compare the two answers.

Where does your truth lie?

Find clarity in your heart's response.

I wish you clarity from the answers of your heart on this Yule night, in the Nights of Yule to come, and ever after.

Ninth Night of Yuletide

December 29/30

❦

Theme: Serenity
Assigned month: September

❦

Serenity is a graceful form of self-awareness.
Marie von Ebner-Eschenbach

Enoch walked faithfully with God;
then he was no more,
because God took him away.
(Genesis 5, 21–24)

This verse from the Christian Bible describes Enoch's ascent into Heaven. Ascension and resurrection mark the end of the cycle of incarnations in this realm and the return, first to the spiritual realms, and later to unite with the Origin, with God. This is the goal of all souls. The prerequisite is the gift of "walking faithfully with God," that is, to desire, allow, and put into practice everything that the heart desires.

Freedom is the freedom of your heart. Choose freedom now and enjoy your happiness. Self-assurance, inner peace, and feeling calm, secure, and contented all lead to serenity, as does being entirely yourself.

And yet we often find ourselves feeling far from serene, despite all our clear insights and intentions. How quickly a single provocative word, a simple questioning of something we have said, or a trivial event can upset our supposed balance. What use is the clarity you have gained, the awareness of your heartfelt desires, their reality, if fear keeps gaining the upper hand?

Fear derives from being aware of the finite, that things come to an end. It could be the end of a relationship, a chapter in your life, or of life itself. If everything has its time, then fear certainly does too, but does fear really have to become "existential"? If something is coming to an end, there will be a (new) beginning at some point, so do not place any limitations on yourself or steer your life toward a dead end.

Why are you afraid of the end of this life when death is merely a pause in the changing scenery on your soul's journey? Relax! Simply being is serenity itself.

Being

Being is
Peace within you,
Peace
When love is
Within everything.

You are, when peace is
Within you.
Being is love.
Love is peace
In your heart.

There is no Being, no protection, no love
Where grief, rage, hatred,
And craving lead you.

Love of hatred
Is lost love
Fallen from Being
Into deceptive Having.

Not being able to let go,
Possessing yourself,
Not Being,
But craving.

Learn to sense yourself,
Whether it takes hours, days
Months, years,
A lifetime.

Being is when it
Is yours and yours alone,
When you feel your heart,
Then the time for love has come.

Among all the tears and anger, you are
Beside yourself.
Let grief be, let anger be,
If their time has come.
Dissolve them away
In the light of your heart.

Being is peace.
Love is
Expression of Being.

Life is the interplay
Of Being.
The Creator is
Love and eternal peace.

At one with ourselves,
Being at one.
Thought, word and deed,
Being achieves itself
In creating
The peace of eternal motion.

Werner Hartung

PRACTICES FOR THE NINTH YULETIDE NIGHT

Here we include practical advice with a choice of optional questions for your Yuletide journal.

LOOKING BACK ON SEPTEMBER OF LAST YEAR

How did I experience the start of fall?

Were there any particular celebrations?

Which people were especially important to me?

Did I go on any journeys?

What was particularly enjoyable?

Who gave me support?

What good things happened to me?

To whom or what should I offer thanks?

Did anything unpleasant happen?

Did I suffer any particular setbacks?

Were there any arguments, conflicts, disappointments?

Is there anyone I haven't yet forgiven?

What situations and experiences during last September would I now like to cleanse or resolve?

What kept upsetting or disturbing my daily routine, my life in general?

In what areas of life did I feel there was a lack of serenity?

In what areas of life would I like to be more relaxed?

REFLECTING ON THE THEME OF THE DAY

Exercise

For once I will be conscious of how I behave toward people during disagreements. I will relive the situation, replaying it in my mind or perhaps going over it again with friends. We can agree on a topic and rules for discussion, see how we react, and then evaluate our responses. I will be aware of what provokes me and how the things that get under my skin can destroy my composure.

I will think about certain behavioral patterns, about feelings and aggression that have bothered me in the past and may do so again in the future. Can I be present, maintain my composure, take someone's opposing point of view seriously and consider it while still retaining my self-control?

Do I notice when unspoken or unconscious issues trigger anxiety and unease, undermine my self-confidence, and shape my judgment of another person's position?

Can I allow myself to think that I am responsible for everything I encounter? That every disagreement is a mirror of what I (often unconsciously) believe, from which I can learn and grow? Can I reach out to others, forgive, and be thankful, even for conflict?

LOOKING AHEAD TO SEPTEMBER IN THE COMING YEAR

Encounters and signs

What did I dream of today?

How was the weather, the general mood, the atmosphere?

What happened today?

Who or what did I encounter during my meditation (situations/ individuals/animals/plants)?

What signs was I shown today?

Did anything happen that indicated serenity?

Consciously shaping the future

What is my vision for this September?

What daydreams did I have today?

In which areas of my life would I like more serenity during the year to come?

A MEDITATION TO DEEPEN THIS EXPERIENCE

Through the power of my heart, I am relaxed.

Today, the door is open to bringing serenity into your life. Can you aspire to allow and achieve everything your heart desires? Can you leave the rest behind?

Freedom is the freedom of your heart. Choose freedom now and enjoy your happiness. Self-assurance, inner peace, and feeling calm, secure, and contented all lead to serenity, as does being you, being entirely yourself.

And yet we often find ourselves feeling far from serene, despite all our clear insights and intentions. How quickly a single provocative word, a simple questioning of something we have said, or a trivial event can upset our supposed balance. What use is the clarity you have gained, the awareness of the reality of your heartfelt desires, if fear keeps gaining the upper hand?

Today, on every day in September, and whenever you feel angry, the door is open to replacing this feeling with composure and calm. Today is calling on you to stand still, pause for a moment, and to be serene. Fill this space of silence and emptiness, this place of power, creation, and creativity, with your serenity. The meditation below will help you to find serenity. Today is the day you plant its seed.

MEDITATION

Make yourself comfortable.

Be aware of your body and how it feels.

Tense and relax your muscles, one at a time.

First your feet, calf muscles, knees, and thighs.

Tense your buttocks, stomach muscles, back, and shoulders.

Tense your fingers, hands, arms, and neck.

Pull a face (grimace) to tense the muscles of your head.

Fill your lungs with fresh oxygen.

Yawn and take a few deep breaths.

Now collect your thoughts and be quiet.

Breathe calmly, easily, and in your own rhythm.

Relax, take composed, quiet breaths.

Place both hands, one on top of the other, over your heart chakra.

Make a connection with your heart.

Feel the warmth and boundless strength that give your body rhythm.

Place your left hand on your heart chakra.

Place your right hand on your solar plexus, just below your ribcage, at the top of your stomach.

Now simply let the power of your heart flow to your solar plexus for a few moments.

Relax, breathe calmly.

Sense how the power of your heart spreads the rhythm of serenity slowly throughout your body.

Now test your heart's strength once more.

Think of a time in the past when you felt disturbed and were very annoyed.

Feel the emotions this still provokes within you, in the pit of your stomach.

Dissolve this energy in the light of your heart by sending out its power.

Let it spread calm and composure throughout your body.

The serenity of your heart helps you to be and stay calm.

May the power of your heart fill you with quietness and peace of mind from now on.

I wish you serenity and strength of heart on this Yule night, in the Nights of Yule to come, and ever after.

Tenth Night of Yuletide

December 30/31

Theme: Journey into a new life
Assigned month: October

A journey of a thousand miles begins with a single step.

Lao Tzu

Get ready today for a new stage on your life's journey, to begin in the New Year or later. When you prepare for a vacation you choose a destination, perhaps one that you have long dreamed about, and imagine what it will be like there, what you might do, whom or what you might encounter.

Traveling involves leaving a place and a way of life behind, giving up home comforts, forgoing a cherished routine, and being open to the new and unexpected. It means a departure from your usual self-assurance, often in an uncertain direction. You won't know what it is like at your destination until you arrive.

You can imagine and dream about what it will be like to travel. When you set off on a new journey, or even decide to resume an existing one, do not let your thoughts return to the past and everything you are leaving behind. Say goodbye to it all and instead savor the anticipation of the new trip.

Embarking on a journey also means limiting yourself to essentials, as well as assessing what is important or necessary to take with you. What can I take with me? What should I take? What weighs me down unnecessarily? What or whom am I leaving behind?

Think of scenarios for fulfilling your most heartfelt wishes. Build up a mental image of them. Be creative on this "inner journey to yourself," break your own boundaries and do not be afraid to let your imagination take flight. Go with any spontaneous thoughts and ideas you may have. They are fleeting, so seize them while you can, but do not run away from your dreams by letting the fear become reality that they may be too wonderful and amazing to come true.

PRACTICES FOR THE TENTH YULETIDE NIGHT

Here we include practical advice with a choice of optional questions for your Yuletide journal.

LOOKING BACK ON OCTOBER OF LAST YEAR

Did I have a good October harvest this year?

Were there any particular celebrations?

Which people were especially important to me?

Did I go on any journeys?

What was particularly enjoyable?

Who gave me support?

What good things happened to me?

To whom or what should I offer thanks?

Did anything unpleasant happen?

Did I suffer any particular setbacks?

Were there any arguments, conflicts, disappointments?

Is there anyone I haven't yet forgiven?

What situations and experiences during last October would I now like to cleanse or resolve?

Which habits had I already decided to change or abandon last year?

What is it time to change now?

What should I leave behind in my partnership, my career, in my internal and external life?

REFLECTING ON THE THEME OF THE DAY

Questions

Have I chosen a destination for my journey?

Am I ready to embark upon my trip?

What should I say goodbye to?

Who might come with me?

What will I pack in my case?

What will I leave behind and what do I want to take with me on my journey into my new life?

A journey within

I will begin my dream journey by sitting or lying down and relaxing. I will go on an inner journey and allow myself to be transported by my thoughts and feelings and the images in my mind.

Providing I can handle my fantasies and daydreams well, I will travel alone. If not, I will ask someone I trust to accompany me while meditating, describing to them the images I see as I go through my inner journey.

They may ask me questions, and, where appropriate, prompt me to continue or help me to refocus if rationality or doubt (hopefully, not the case) start to intrude, or if I do not know what to do next.

I will make no special preparations, but I will wish for a companion or guide. Perhaps a traveling companion will appear, a loved one, a sympathetic stranger, or a power animal. I will go with them, without fear, and allow myself to be led away. Such is life. My friend may take notes or I will make my own notes later about what happened on the dream journey.

LOOKING AHEAD TO OCTOBER IN THE COMING YEAR

Encounters and signs

What dreams did I have today?

How was the weather, the general mood, the atmosphere?

What happened today?

Who or what did I encounter during my meditation (situations/ individuals/animals/plants)?

What signs was I shown today?

What indications and signs did I receive concerning my journey into a new life?

Where is my journey taking me?

Were there any indications regarding achievable life goals for the coming year?

Consciously shaping the future

What is my vision for this coming October?

What daydreams did I have today?

What insights have I gained through my experiences in the last Nights of Yuletide?

What would I like to finally leave behind and where would I like my life to take me during the year to come?

A MEDITATION TO DEEPEN THIS EXPERIENCE

I am taking a journey into my new life. An inner journey.

Today, the door is open for a journey into your new life. Today, you will be packing your suitcase for this journey into your new life and your new year. You will not know what it is really like until you get there. Leave behind everything that is in the past. Bid it farewell and start looking forward to your trip.

Today, on every October day, and whenever you want to start something new, the door is open for the journey into your new life.

Today is calling on you to stand still, pause for a moment, and be perfectly calm. Fill this space of silence and emptiness, this place of power, of creation, and creativity, with everything you take with you on this journey into your new life.

The following meditation will guide your inner journey. Plant the seed for it in your life today.

MEDITATION

Yes, it is possible to take a trial journey into your new life.

There is no need to book a ticket, make a payment, or even pack your case.

All you have to do is make yourself comfortable.

Close your eyes and choose the destination.

Perhaps it is a goal you have already set for your new life.

Or perhaps you will leave the choice of both route and destination to those who accompany you on your journey.

Place complete trust in whatever you are now about to encounter.

Do not have an agenda, but instead be open to whatever is about to happen.

Calmly observe what is happening in your mind's eye.

Is someone coming to meet you?

A person or a power animal?

Follow them, along whatever path they might take you and wherever they might lead.

Now slowly return from the reality of your inner journey to the present.

Think how you were affected by the images you saw on the journey.

Consider how they made you feel, the impressions they made on you.

You can now return there at any time.

I wish you pleasant travels, whatever journey you embark upon, and an exciting life journey on this Yule night, in the Nights of Yule to come, and ever after.

Eleventh Night of Yuletide

December 31/January 1
(New Year's Eve and New Year's Day)

— ◈ —

Theme: Explore your feelings anew
Assigned month: November

— ◈ —

Perplexity is the beginning of knowledge.
Khalil Gibran

Today, look back at the first ten days of your contemplative and spiritual journey during the interval between the years. Review the various outcomes so far and build them into an image that will guide you. How do you feel about what you have encountered in the Nights of Yuletide to date? The eve of the transition into the new year is a good time to take stock of yourself emotionally. Or, to put it another way, to take stock of the new version of yourself that may have taken shape over the last few days. If some aspects of this new you are in fact not all that new, then the results will at least be a confirmation of yourself.

Think again about your plans and possible choices and see how you really feel about them. Is it really you? Is this what you want to be or become? A new you, or do you prefer the old you?

Reexamining your feelings is about finding assurance, self-assurance.

Assurance

Do you feel the love of your heart?
The never-ending kiss of your soul
Feeding the fire of your deeds there?

Do you feel yourself nestling in the love of the Earth
Whose child you are and who lends you
Her warm coat
While you are a guest here?

Do you feel the one eternal love within you
Protecting and enveloping you as the
Endless Source that springs eternal from
Your own heart?

Do you feel sheltered in the raiment of the Earth,
The ineffable depths
Of the ocean and the Cosmos?

Do you draw on the depths
Of your soul
To enrich the world?

Then you are sure of yourself.
Security is based only on self-assurance.
You cannot possess or demand security,
You can only be sure of yourself or of another.

Use your feelings to explore
If the other person is also sure
Of themselves.
You will share the eternal kiss
Of your heart with them, receive their kiss
And experience inseparability.

Werner Hartung

PRACTICES FOR THE ELEVENTH YULETIDE NIGHT

Here we include practical advice with a choice of optional questions for your Yuletide journal.

LOOKING BACK ON NOVEMBER OF LAST YEAR

Was I consciously aware of the days getting shorter?

Were there any particular celebrations?

Which people were especially important to me?

Did I go on any journeys?

What was particularly nice?

Who gave me support?

What good things happened to me?

To what or whom should I offer thanks?

Did anything unpleasant happen?

Did I suffer any particular setbacks?

Were there any arguments, conflicts, disappointments?

Is there anyone I haven't yet forgiven?

What situations and experiences during last November would I now like to cleanse or resolve?

REFLECTING ON THE THEME OF THE DAY

Reflections

Am I happy with all the all the emotions and insights, all the goals, resolutions, and decisions that came to me during the Nights of Yuletide? Today, I am going to prioritize my feelings. Have I managed to dispel my anxieties and doubts? Am I starting to feel good about things, are the first rays of sun (or even a shooting star) bringing light to the still dark days? I will try to describe my feelings in images.

I will fill myself with myself. I will focus on my feelings, what I now wish to be and what I am.

The end of an old year and the beginning of a new one are causes for joyful celebration. Today, I will consciously devote myself to this celebration and to the joys of life, perhaps with a good meal, dancing, music, but also with a lightness of heart. There is always something exciting, something thrilling about a new beginning, which often prompts the raising of a glass to toast things to come. I will say goodbye to everything I want to leave behind with a flourish, letting off my own fireworks and illuminating the darkness with a dreamlike glow.

LOOKING AHEAD TO NOVEMBER IN THE COMING YEAR

Encounters and signs

What dreams did I have today?

How was the weather, the general mood, the atmosphere?

What happened today?

Who or what did I encounter during my meditation (situations/individuals/animals/plants)?

What signs was I shown today?

What indications and signs did I receive relating to my feelings and the year to come?

Consciously shaping the future

What is my vision for this November?

What daydreams did I have today?

What do I visualize for the coming year?

A MEDITATION TO DEEPEN THIS EXPERIENCE

I feel my sense of fulfillment growing. Security.

Today, the door is open to making your wishes come true. The great thing about life is that it is like a play, set on a living stage that is just waiting to be filled with all our energy, desires, and fantasies. Creating visions for the future and finding self-confidence on this living stage represent freedom and joy for us. Today, on every November day, and whenever you are truly aware of your desires, the door to fulfillment is open.

Today is calling on you to stand still, pause for a moment, and think carefully about how you are feeling and what you want. Fill this space of silence and emptiness, this place of power, creation, and creativity, with your desires.

The following meditation will help. Today is the day you plant the seed of fulfillment in your life.

MEDITATION

Place your hands on your heart chakra.

Do you feel the love of your heart?

The never-ending kiss of your soul that feeds the fire of your actions?

Do you feel cradled in the love of the Earth?

You are its child and it lends you its warm coat while you are a guest here.

Do you feel the one eternal love within you?

Surrounding and protecting you as a source that springs eternal from your own heart?

Now feel safely wrapped in the Earth's coat.

The unfathomable depths of the ocean and of space create the things with which you will enrich the world from the depths of your soul.

You will then be sure of yourself.

Only self-assurance can underpin security.

You cannot simply have or demand security.

You can only be sure of yourself and of others.

I wish you the security of being certain of yourself and your desires on this Yule night, in the Nights of Yule to come, and ever after.

Twelfth Night of Yuletide

January 1/2

Theme: Be creative in shaping and achieving the life you want
Assigned month: December

*Each of us bears a productive uniqueness within him as the core of his being;
and when he becomes aware of it, there appears around him a strange
penumbra which is the mark of his singularity.*

Friedrich Nietzsche

Many a good self-help guide tells us to focus our thoughts on a single goal, which is indeed key to success in shaping and manifesting the life we want.

Focus on and examine your thoughts and see what goal they inspire. This is the only way to create the necessary resonances in the outside world to achieve what you seek. However, there is no point in dreaming of your goal unless it is followed by action. For example, if you want to be a healer, it is not sufficient just to make the decision. You must buy a treatment table, equip and furnish a room appropriately, and let people know that you ready to offer healing. The initial thought "places the order," giving voice to your idea starts the ball rolling, but it is not until you take action that it becomes reality. And you do want to achieve your goal, don't you?

Be aware of how you can generate resonances on two key planes. One plane is among your fellow humans, who will react to you according to the aura you send out. If their reaction does not match your expectations, think about whether your vibrations are perhaps not yet as "pure" as you would like them to be, causing dissonance and even discord. Think about why this might be and discuss it with people you trust.

The second plane is within the universe. It is the power of your love and thoughts and how these are implemented that creates realities from the primordial material of the twelve basic forces. If you have inner clarity and harmony of thought, word, and deed, then the universe will provide you with everything you need for the new direction your heart is taking.

Use this last Night of Yuletide to organize yourself and ultimately to fix the three-fold process of creation (see page 139) in your consciousness. By tomorrow you will already have returned to your normal daily life.

PRACTICES FOR THE TWELFTH YULETIDE NIGHT

Here we include practical advice with a choice of optional questions for your Yuletide journal.

LOOKING BACK ON DECEMBER OF LAST YEAR

Was I consciously aware of the Advent period, the days of the Christmas holidays, the Nights of Yule?

Were there any other particular occasions to celebrate?

Which people were especially important to me?

Did I go on any journeys?

What was particularly enjoyable?

Who gave me support?

What good things happened to me?

To whom or what should I offer thanks?

Did anything unpleasant happen?

Did I suffer any particular setbacks?

Were there any arguments, conflicts, disappointments?

Is there anyone I have yet to forgive?

What situations and experiences during last December would I now like to cleanse or resolve?

In what circumstances did I creatively draw strength from my heart in three ways (thought, word, deed)?

In what circumstances did I become caught up in thoughts and words, without taking action?

REFLECTING ON THE THEME OF THE DAY

Reassuring myself

I will make a brief summary of my plan and my heartfelt desires, as if I were giving a presentation to a room of people, to demonstrate my conviction that I "am" the plan I am putting forward. I will use short, concise sentences to summarize my goals and create a "mind map" with a drawing, painting, or collage. I will allow my imagination free rein but without losing sight of my objectives: clarity, truth, and succinctness. If I have confidence in myself and my plans, I can do this. I only have myself to convince—I am my own worst critic and greatest supporter at the same time. But then, this is *my* life, and it is unique.

Banishing doubt

On what occasions have I seen my desires fall "on fertile ground"? When have I seen my wishes come true through the strength of my heart or thoughts, my belief and trust, my self-confidence? What past good experiences can I revisit, taking up again where I left off to give myself courage and strength for new things? I will make a note of some of these situations, fix them in my mind, and internalize them.

LOOKING AHEAD TO DECEMBER IN THE COMING YEAR

Encounters and signs

What dreams did I have today?

How was the weather, the general mood, the atmosphere?

What happened today?

Who or what did I encounter during my meditation (situations/ individuals/animals/plants)?

What signs was I shown today?

What indications and signs did I receive that relate to creative manifestation in my life in the coming year?

Consciously shaping the future

What is my vision for this December?

What daydreams did I have today?

In what areas of life would I like to be a creative manifestor in the year to come and what areas are of particular importance to me?

A MEDITATION TO DEEPEN THIS EXPERIENCE

What I want also wants me. I bless my creative powers with the power of the elements: sun, water, air, and earth. A blessing.

Today, the door is open to empowering your creativity, your creative wealth, to fulfilling your ideas and desires, and to blessing the seeds you have planted so far in life.

Today, on every December day, and whenever something new in your life begins, the door is open to blessings for abundant growth and a rich harvest.

Today is calling on you to stand still, pause for a moment, and to be completely calm. Fill this space of silence and emptiness, this place of power, creation, and creativity, with the blessings of Heaven and Earth, with the blessings of fire, living water, air, and earth. Plant the seed of blessing in your life today. The following meditation (which can also be spoken aloud as a prayer) will support you, as water sustains a plowed field.

Now, thank the powers of Creation that stand at your side, so that a strong plant will grow from the seed you have planted and whose fruit you will soon be able to harvest. Ask for the blessing of the four elements: the fire of the sun, the coolness of water, the freshness of air, and the fertility of earth.

MEDITATION

Angel of the sun!

There is no warmth without you,

no fire without you,

no life without you.

The green leaves of the trees worship you,

and it is through you that tiny grains of wheat become

a sea of golden stalks,
swaying in the wind.
The flower at the center of my body
is opened through you.
Angel of the sun,
holy messenger of Mother Earth,
enter my holy temple
and give me the fire of life!

Yes, we worship you, Water of Life.
The waters flow from the Heavenly Seas,
springing from sources that never run dry.
A thousand pure springs,
mists, and clouds
run in my blood.
And all the waters made by the Creator are holy.

Angel of water,
holy messenger of Mother Earth,
enter the blood that flows within me.
Wash my body in the rain,
that falls from the sky
and give me the Water of Life.

The highest, eternal place of light
where countless stars hold sway
is the air we breathe in
and the air we breathe out.

And all the mysteries of the boundless garden
lie hidden in the moment
between breathing in and breathing out.

Angel of air,
holy messenger of Mother Earth,
blow deep within me,
so that I can learn the secrets of the wind
and the music of the stars.

I praise the broad earth,
its generous spaces, its many paths,
the fruitful bounty it produces,
your mother, holy plant!
Those who sow corn, grasses, and fruits
are sowing Divine Order.
May they have a bounteous harvest.
Sweet and plentiful riches shall spring forth
from this land, from the fields,
bringing health and healing,
nourishment and vitality.

Angel of Earth, make my seed fruitful,
and give my body life with your power!
May you have success in patiently growing the seed you have
planted.
Enjoy it and look forward to the harvest.

This I wish you during this Night of Yule, and ever after . . .

Returning to Your Daily Routine

January 2/3

Theme: Embracing and enjoying life

There are twelve basic forces in the universe and twelve months in the year. Over the course of twelve steps in twelve days, you have come closer to yourself, rediscovered and reshaped or reconfirmed yourself. The number thirteen is the number of unity (three in one and one in three). When unity is divided, three is created, as one finds its mirror image, its manifestation. Creation is a threefold process consisting of thought, word, and deed, symbolized by a triangle or a pyramid.

You, too, are a creative being within the matrix revealed to you by the Creator. Turn your gaze outward once more, reveal what springs from your heart.

As this Thirteenth day dawns, you will find yourself back in your familiar "reality." Cast your mind back to what you have experienced, felt, and learned during the Nights of Yuletide. Embrace it one more time and then return to your normal life.

PRACTICES FOR THE RETURN

On the eve of your new beginning, take another look through the notes you made in your journal. Once you feel centered and grounded, you will be able to achieve a great deal, although perhaps not everything. Expect some setbacks, as things may not immediately go to plan. And leave space in your plans for fate to play a part. You do not have to—and in any case cannot—control everything. So do not try, but instead look forward with anticipation to what you are likely to encounter. How else might you be pleasantly surprised?

Questions

What do I wish to change this year in terms of my behavior toward others in my family or in the workplace?

What goals for self-development shall I pursue this year?

How do I want to embark upon January?

What do I want to end now and to begin?

Which obstacles do I need to remove to achieve these aims?

What material challenges are there?

How might people react to my transformation?

Affirmations

I expect to face tests in my normal everyday life right from the start, tests that will challenge my ambitions and the way I hope to behave. I resolve to pause at such moments and take short breaks in which I can take a few deep breaths, relax, and reassure myself. I will then recall and return to my plans for the future once more.

I will take pleasure in each successful step I take, but I *will not* get angry and I *will not* criticize myself if something fails to work out straightaway. I am learning to forgive myself.

I am open to the surprises that life will bring, to the people and situations that inspire me to learn and teach others. I am ready for spiritual growth.

I am learning to set, recognize, and respect boundaries. I thank and forgive those who teach me, just as I thank and forgive those whose paths now depart from mine.

FINAL THOUGHTS ON RETURNING TO YOUR DAILY ROUTINE

Today is the day you will find your way back to your normal life. You have opened up many possibilities and options for your future with the exercises and meditations in this book. I would like to encourage you to allow life to surprise you from now on, while in the immediate future, you can focus on what you have achieved through your work with these exercises.

From today (and ideally, every day), make a note of two or three things that you have made possible for yourself.

Make a note every day of one or two things for which you can be thankful. This will help you to keep your focus on what you enjoy, and life will always bring you things for which you can be thankful. Be aware of all the gifts and surprises that your life has in store for you.

It is so nice that you have come through this door with us!

We thank you for your trust,

And we hope you start your journey full of confidence
as you follow your path into your new life.

Anne Stallkamp, Werner Hartung

Starting Out

The nightingale
Has long since fallen silent;
The stars are fading.

When the storm
Abates,
The blackbird
Will begin its solo song.

The bird kingdom's chorus
Starts softly.
Always the same.

But each day,
There is a new song.
May you draw confidence
From this assurance.

Werner Hartung

ABOUT THE AUTHORS

Anne Stallkamp has been working with Werner Hartung since 2010 on developing new approaches to geomancy and geomantic astrology, and conducting training courses in geomancy and spiritual healing. She is also a qualified interior designer and integrates energetic balancing and the clearing of living areas and workspaces into her commissions. She is a geomantic practitioner, healer, Reiki master, and teacher, and the mother of an adult son. Anne and Werner married in 2013 and they now live in Hanover, Germany.

Werner Hartung founded his first practice for spiritual healing in 2004 and started to develop new approaches to geomancy. His abilities with energy and as a medium have retrieved much forgotten knowledge for us and brought healing to people, animals, and the Earth. He leads training courses in geomancy, spiritual healing, and channeling workshops, and works with Anne to carry out clearing and the energetic balancing of living and working environments. He is the father of two adult children and a spiritual healer, geomantic practitioner, author, Reiki master, and teacher.

Picture Credits
Ornamental snowflakes for chapter headings:
Based on W.A. Bentley and
W.J. Humphreys, *Snow Crystals* (1931)
Ornamental snowflake on pages 113, 121, and 129:
vectorstock.com

For further information and to request a book catalog contact:
Inner Traditions, One Park Street, Rochester, Vermont 05767

Earthdancer Books is an Inner Traditions imprint
Phone: +1-800-246-8648, customerservice@innertraditions.com
www.earthdancerbooks.com • www.innertraditions.com

AN INNER TRADITIONS IMPRINT